Job

"For I know that my Redeemer lives, and at the last He will stand upon the earth. And after my skin has been thus destroyed, yet in my flesh I shall see God."

Job 19:25–26

CONCORDIA PUBLISHING HOUSE · SAINT LOUIS

Edited by Robert C. Baker

This publication may be available in braille, in large print, or on cassette tape for the visually impaired. Please allow 8 to 12 weeks for delivery. Write to the Lutheran Blind Mission, 7550 Watson Rd., St. Louis, MO 63119-4409; call toll-free 1-888-215-2455; or visit the Web site: www.blindmission.org.

Manufactured in the United States of America

2 3 4 5 6 7 8 9 10 11   19 18 17 16 15 14 13 12 11 10

Contents

History	Date (B.C.)	Job
Tell Asmar (Iraq) has smelted iron blade[1]	ca. 2800	
Cheops and Mendure pyramids (Egypt) contain iron tools[1]	ca. 2500	
Abraham born	2166	
	2000–later	Possible dates of historical person Job
Jacob and Esau born	2006	
Abraham dies	1991	
Joseph born	1915	
Hittites (Anatolia; now Turkey) develop iron implements[2]	1900–later	*Iron* mentioned in Job 19:24; 20:24; 28:2; 40:18; 41:27.
Jacob settles in Egypt	1876	
Hammurabi creates Babylonian law code	1755	
Moses born	1526	
Exodus from Egypt	1446	
Middle East widely uses iron; smelting furnaces in Israel[2]	1300–later	
Deborah judges Israel	1209–1169	
Samuel born	1105	
Reign of Saul	1050–1010	
Reign of David	1010–970	
Reign of Solomon	970–930	Luther's suggested date for writing of Job

---

[1] *The International Standard Bible Encyclopedia*, Volume Two: E–J, Geoffrey W. Bromily, gen. ed., (Grand Rapids: Eerdmans, 1982) p. 880.
[2] *The New Encyclopedia Britannica*, Macropaedia, Volume 9, Helen Hemingway Benton, pub., (Chicago: Encyclopedia Britannica, 1972), p. 894.

An Outline of Job

Job follows a three-part, prose-poetry-prose outline form used by several cultures in the ancient Near East. The opening prologue (chs. 1–2) and closing epilogue (42:7–17) are separated by three rounds of dialogue between Job and three friends seeking to "comfort" him, and three monologues ending in God's call for Job to leave difficult and perplexing issues in God's hands. An outline of the book is as follows:

I.   Prologue (1:1–2:13)
     A. Job's Happy Life (1:1–5)
     B. Satan's Accusations and Job's Affliction (1:6–2:13)
II. Dialogues and Monologues (3:1–42:6)
     A. Job's Curse and Complaint (3:1–26)
     B. First Round of Dialogues (4:1–14:22)
        1. Eliphaz's First Speech (4:1–5:27)
        2. Job's First Reply (6:1–7:21)
        3. Bildad's First Speech (8:1–22)
        4. Job's Second Reply (9:1–10:22)
        5. Zophar's First Speech (11:1–20)
        6. Job's Third Reply (12:1–14:22)
     C. Second Round of Dialogues (15:1–21:34)
        1. Eliphaz's Second Speech (15:1–35)
        2. Job's Fourth Reply (16:1–17:16)
        3. Bildad's Second Speech (18:1–21)
        4. Job's Fifth Reply (19:1–29)
        5. Zophar's Second Speech (20:1–29)
        6. Job's Sixth Reply (21:1–34)
     D. Third Round of Dialogues (22:1–31:40)
        1. Eliphaz's Third Speech (22:1–30)
        2. Job's Seventh Reply (23:1–24:25)
        3. Bildad's Third Speech (25:1–6)
        4. Job's Eighth Reply (26:1–27:23)
     E. Praise of Wisdom (28:1–28)

Introduction

I heard upon his dry dung heap
That man cry out who cannot sleep:
"If God is God He is not good,
If God is good He is not God;
Take the even, take the odd,
I would not sleep here if I could. "

—Nickles, from *J.B.,*
a play by Archibald MacLeish

That's how the problem of suffering is explained by Nickles, the Satan character in the play about Job by Pulitzer Prize–winner Archibald MacLeish. Nickles smugly tells God what most folks on earth think of Him: If there is a God, He can't be good; otherwise He wouldn't allow suffering. Or else, if God is good, He isn't powerful enough to do anything about it.

Then strutting before "God's" throne, Nickles/Satan gloats. He has convinced most of humanity that God does not have their good in mind. As though laying down a trump card, he announces the irony of it all. "Father of Lies they call me, don't they?"

If we are like Job, however, we also tend to forget that it's Satan behind our suffering, not God. Part of that might be due to the religious climate of our North American society. It's the very same theology held by Job's friends: If God loves you, He will prosper you. But if you are suffering, it is a sign that you have sinned and God is punishing you. Sound familiar?

The Book of Job shows Job's struggle: Everything he knew about a loving God conflicted with his experience. How could a loving God let this happen to him? Sound familiar?

Job found no easy solutions or pat answers. You won't either. But you will find a surprisingly loving God and Rescuer—just as Job did. My prayer is that this Bible study will help.

My thanks to Pastor Richard Kurth (Houston, Texas) and Pastor David Anderson (Hutchinson, Minnesota), who laid the foundation for this course. And a great big "Thank you" to Dr. Christopher Mitchell of Concordia Publishing House who lent me his insights into the Hebrew tongue and the theology of this profound book.

+ Soli Deo Gloria+

—Dirk van der Linde

Tips on the Book of Job

Here are some background and reading tips to help make your study of this biblical book easier:

1. The true story of Job is one of the oldest in the Bible, taking place perhaps some 2,000 years before Christ and some 500 years before Moses. Some of the Hebrew words are unknown in any other work and are of uncertain meaning.

2. Most of the Book of Job is poetry, and for that reason it is included with the other poetic books of the Old Testament, such as Psalms and Proverbs.

3. Although Hebrew culture did not produce drama as we know it, it may help to think of Job as drama. Yet this drama is played on two stages; it is like watching two plays at the same time. On the upper stage, seated on a throne, is God. In and out before Him come the angels, and Satan. There is conflict between God and Satan over Job's faithfulness.

4. On the lower stage are Job and his friends, primarily Eliphaz, Bildad, and Zophar. (Later comes young Elihu.) Although they come to comfort Job, their religious-sounding advice is worldly. They claim to speak for God, but they don't.

5. The three friends of Job are convinced that Job is suffering because he sinned. They believe that only the wicked suffer. Nevertheless, although Job is a sinner (and he never says he isn't), he is also a redeemed child of God, and he insists that he is innocent—forgiven! The Book of Job will make no sense to anyone who cannot see that the "innocent" can suffer.

6. What Job's friends say about God punishing the wicked does not apply to Job. They speak Law, not the Gospel that would comfort Job. Much of what Job says is confused, angry, and also in error. He incorrectly thinks God is punishing him. The statements of Job and his friends are their opinions, and not necessarily true. But the Lord finally does speak and reveal His grace and truth.

Lesson 1

The Pain and the Puzzle

Pieces of the Puzzle

Here is a puzzle: How can a kind and loving God allow terrible things to happen to a good and faithful person? That was Job's problem. He couldn't figure out God.

But this is not just Job's problem. It is a problem whenever suffering strikes any of God's faithful people. For many of us, Job's story will hit very close to home.

Ask several volunteers to read about Job's first affliction in Job 1. You may wish to divide up the text among several readers.

After reading Job 1–2, answer the following:

1. What are your first reactions to Job's story? Share with the members of your group, especially if this is the first time you have read the Book of Job.

Although you may not know any person who lost all his or her children and material possessions at the same time, share a few details about someone you know who has suffered a loss recently. Without mentioning names, tell how that person was like or unlike Job.

Puzzle Piece #1: Is God, God?

To those who do not believe in God, suffering should be no puzzle at all. They view suffering as merely what comes from living in a universe that is on its own. These people may feel wronged by life's injustice. But since no one is running the universe, how can anyone be held responsible? How can you complain about life's hurts if no one is in control?

Without God, there are plenty of explanations for suffering. But there is no puzzle.

For the Christian, however, it is better and worse than that. It is better because we do have a God to turn to. But it is worse because we have to ask how God can allow us to suffer. That's our first puzzle.

2. Discuss the proposed answers to this puzzle offered below. Which of these have you heard before? Why do, or why don't, these proposed answers solve the puzzle of suffering?

A. *There Is No God:* The reality of evil in the world proves that there is no God powerful enough or willing to stop it. Only what can be scientifically seen and examined is real (atheism/naturalism).

B. *God Is a Myth:* The Bible is not literally or historically true but contains "truths" for our lives. All miracles (including Jesus' incarnation and resurrection) did not actually happen but are expressions of human hopes (higher criticism).

C. *God Is Inside Me:* Like "the Force" in the Star Wars movies, God is a power I can tap into; He is there to help me accomplish what I want in life (New Age theology).

D. *God Is Limited:* The rabbi who wrote *Why Bad Things Happen to Good People* describes a God who is limited by nature's laws. Since God is not all-powerful, He is not able to completely stop evil.

E. Others? What other possible explanations have you heard?

As you undoubtedly noticed, all of the explanations listed above present a limited, restricted God—if they allow the existence of God at all. Although some people may believe in these versions of God, they fall far short of the God who reveals Himself in Scripture, and in particular in the Book of Job.

Read Job 1:8–12, 2:3–6.

3. Both texts show conversations between God and Satan concerning Job. What specific wording shows that God is in complete control of the situation?

4. Twice Satan tells God that He should strike Job with His own hand (1:11, 2:5). Yet in both cases, how does God reply (1:12, 2:6)?

5. Even though Job was struck with evil, how do we know that God was still in full control of the situation? (Reread 1:12, 2:6.)

6. Job was under attack. Yet the source of attack was Satan, not God. In light of that insight, which of the following responses comes closest to your opinion? (You are not restricted to only one response.)

a. "Pain is pain. So what difference does where it comes from make?"

b. "Suffering is easier to take if I know it's not from God's hand."

c. "So what if God isn't the source of suffering? Why doesn't He stop it?"

d. Other responses?

Theories that restrict God and His power really do not help us understand the problem of suffering after all. Why not? Because they are not rooted in truth. God is. And God is God. That means He is all-powerful; He is in control. That does not mean we have solved the problem of pain—far from it. We have to explore the second piece of the puzzle.

Puzzle Piece #2: Is God Good?

We get to "overhear" the conversation between Satan and God concerning Job. Interestingly, Job did not. Therefore, Job doesn't really know the cause (and the causer) of his suffering, and he believes God is punishing him. That is why throughout the book Job repeatedly asks, *Why are You doing this to me, God?*

This brings us to the second puzzle piece. If God is all-powerful and able to stop suffering, then why doesn't He? Wouldn't a good and loving God do so? This question is getting down to the basics: What kind of God do we have anyway?

Read the following proposals for this piece of the puzzle. These are summarized opinions and views taken from a variety of philosophies and writings.

A. *Two gods?* Dualism, the belief in two gods, one good and one evil, used to be very popular (e.g., Zoroastrianism). Because neither God nor Satan (if he is the evil god) has all the power, good doesn't

16

always win out over evil. Some trace of this dualism can be found in New Age theology.

B. *Aloof God?* Called deism, this view of God was believed by such men as Thomas Jefferson and Benjamin Franklin. Deism teaches a God so transcendent (above us) that He does not concern Himself with human affairs. Although God created the world, He is indifferent and uncaring, and we are left in this world alone, without Him.

C. *Other?* Combinations of these and other beliefs can be found in abundance. List some other views you may have heard.

Again, these alternate views of God, and what He is like, fall short of the God who reveals Himself in Scripture. As we will see, Job's problem (and ours!) was not that God was no more powerful than evil, nor that God was aloof and indifferent.

Job's problem was that God is good—holy, in fact. Unbelievably, it was a good and holy God that allowed evil to happen! And what made Job's problem even worse was not that God was aloof and indifferent. Quite to the contrary, God wouldn't get off Job's case (this was Job's opinion). God was hounding Job.

7. Read Job 9:1–14. This shows Job's knowledge of God and what He is like. On a board or newsprint flip chart, list some of God's powerful works that Job describes. Why does this revelation of what God is like leave no room for dualism or deism?

8. Reread Job 9:2, and continue with 9:14–20. This text is not easy! Although Job is complaining against God, he is not accusing God of evil. He is merely charging that God isn't good toward him. Which of the following best describes Job's thought and feelings? Give reasons for your answer based on the text.

a. Job believes that since God is good, all he has to do is wait patiently and God will give him what he wants.

b. Job is bitter and angry at God; he wants nothing to do with Him.

17

c. Job is hurt, bitter, and confused by God's ways; he feels he has been treated unjustly. He wants answers.

d. Other.

Read Job 10:1–3, 8–12. It's as though Job is saying, "God is acting in ways He ought not act!" Job knows God to be good, but he does not see God acting that way toward himself.

9. Reread verses 8–12. Although it seems Job is almost falling into disbelief, here he remembers God's work of creation—especially the very personal creation of the man Job. How does Job picture the God of creation? good or evil? caring or indifferent? Give reasons for your answer.

10. Job knows with certainty two things about God. But those two things collide and clash. God is good, yes. God is almighty, yes. In creation, God acted both with goodness and might. But now, why should God want to destroy something He created with such love? That's Job's question.

a. Job does not doubt that God is good; he just doubts the goodness of God toward himself. Is Job wrong, or sinning, by doubting God's goodness?

b. What would you tell Job if you were one of his friends?

Puzzle Piece #3: Is Job Good?

Could the problem of Job's suffering lie with Job himself? Although outwardly a godly man, could he be harboring some secret sin? Is his suffering God's way of flushing this sin out into the open? If so, then the puzzle of pain is solved, and everything fits together very nicely. Then suffering is God's punishment for our sins. People only suffer because they deserve it. God is fair and just in accordance with His Law (not gracious and merciful according to the Gospel).

If so, then Job's three friends are correct. Their strongly worded messages carry one prominent theme: "Job, you have sinned. Stop whining about all the wrong you suffered. Instead, repent!"

If only it were that simple!

We will delve far more deeply into this piece of the puzzle in the next session. For now, however, see whether or not the friends of Job, and their view, line up with God and His view of Job.

Reread Job 1:1, 8; and 2:3.

11. These texts are God's words and description of the man Job. Although the answer is fairly obvious, does God's view of Job blend with the friends' view? Why or why not?

12. Some scholars maintain that although Job was "blameless," he still loved his wealth more than he loved God. Others add that Job was self-centered, if not self-righteous. They maintain that while Job did not sin in what he said (see Job 2:10), he sinned in his heart. Therefore, they say, his suffering was good because it made Job turn to God as he never did before.

a. On the basis of God's description of Job (see text listed above), do you think there is support for these scholars' theories? Explain your answer.

b. By calling Job self-righteous these scholars make Job sound like one of the Pharisees of Jesus' day. From what you know of Job so far, how is he like/unlike the Pharisees?

13. Some say that suffering is good because it brings us closer to God. Do you agree or disagree? Explain your answer. (We will discuss this further in another session.)

14. Job was blameless in the sense that he trusted in God's grace, was forgiven, and lived by faith. But he never claimed to be sinless. Why is that distinction important? Do you think God punishes people (such as Job) because they are not sinless? Explain your answer.

Gathering the Pieces—for Now

We have not solved the puzzle of pain. In this introductory session, we have simply looked at some of the pieces of the puzzle. And we have done all this, really, from Job's point of view. Not God's. Not yet.

In the Book of Job, God doesn't even begin to explain His view until the end (Job 38–41). But we do not need to wait until the end to get a strong hint of what God's answer to the puzzle of pain might be.

God's strongest answer comes in the form of His own Son, Christ Jesus, the Word of God made flesh (John 1:14). For a glimpse at how Jesus answers the problem and puzzle of suffering, read Matthew 16:21–28.

15. Share a time when you might have been in a suffering situation (even if it wasn't as severe as Job's). Did you view God as

Job did? Did you think God was punishing you? How does Jesus' suffering help you when you suffer?

In Closing

Encourage participants to begin the following activities:
* If you haven't done so already, read Job 1–2.
* Recite responsively a psalm-like text in another Old Testament book, Isaiah 43:1–13. As you read the words God is speaking to His people, imagine how Job, or any other sufferer, might respond.
* Read Job 3–9 to prepare for the next lesson.

Close with prayer.

Lesson 2

Looking into Secret Sins
Part 1

Catching God's Signals?

Imagine how you would feel if a friend accused you of wrongdoing when you were down, like Eliphaz spoke to Job: "You're suffering? Well, obviously you must have done something very wicked, and God is punishing you for it now." How can a friend say such a thing?

Perhaps none of your friends are as blunt as Eliphaz. But Eliphaz's way of looking at things is shared by countless people. It is based on the idea that God blesses and prospers good people, and curses and punishes bad people. If you twist that idea even further, you might believe that prosperity and good health are signs from God that you are a good person and that God loves you. Even worse, you might think that poverty, disease, or other misfortunes are signs from God that you are a wicked person and that He no longer loves you.

16. Divide into small groups. Within your group ask a volunteer to read the following comments. These were actual statements spoken by real people at times of crisis. With which comments do you agree? disagree? Give reasons for your answer. Share whether you have ever heard comments such as these. How would you reply?

"Your mother would have survived her cancer if she'd just had more faith and prayed harder."

"Our baby probably died because God knew we would not be good parents for him."

"Of course I didn't want him to get killed, but he probably brought it down on himself. I guess he got what he deserved."

"Everything in my life is going wrong—and I don't even know what I'm doing that is so bad."

"Maybe God gave me this disease to teach me some patience."

Reassemble the small groups into one large group. Let each small group share one of the comments and their reply.

Secret Sins?

As you have just seen, there are many modern-day versions of Job's friends. They, too, give out explanations for evil and advice for what sufferers must do. To understand better what lies behind the thinking of Job's friends (and their modern counterparts!), let's allow them to speak for themselves. Ask a volunteer to read Job 4:1–21. These are the words of Job's first friend, Eliphaz.

You may wish to divide into small groups to discuss the following prompts.

17. Reread verses 3–5. Although Eliphaz begins by complimenting Job, he turns the compliment into a criticism. For what is

Eliphaz criticizing Job? In your view, is it a valid criticism? Why or why not?

18. It is not that good people will never suffer! But Eliphaz believes that good people can expect quick rescue from God because God helps the good and hinders the bad. Reread verse 6.

a. According to Eliphaz, why can Job expect a quick rescue from God? Do you think Eliphaz is correct? Give reasons for your answer.

b. How will Eliphaz's view of Job change if God's rescue is not speedy? How do people today respond toward those whose suffering is lengthy?

19. Reread verses 7–9. Eliphaz says he has never seen an exception to "you reap what you sow." On a scale of 1 to 10 (1 being rare, 10 being very common), how widespread is this "you get what you deserve" philosophy among people today?

20. Eliphaz seems to have a point. Although written at a much different time, Eliphaz's words in 4:7–9 sound similar to Psalm 37:25, 27; 1 Peter 3:10–12; and Galatians 6:7–8. Why are Eliphaz's words misleading, while the psalm and the words of Peter and Paul are correct? We will cover this question in more detail in a later session.

21. People who hold Eliphaz's view firmly believe that God always rewards good and punishes evil during this life. They believe, therefore, that long-term suffering must be a sign of God's displeasure. The sufferer must be sinning. What Eliphaz says next is frightening.

a. Because he and the other two friends can never point to any specific sin in Job, how does he claim to know that Job is sinning? (See 4:12, 15.) Why is Eliphaz's claim so dangerous?

b. Perhaps you or someone in your group received advice from a well-meaning friend who claimed a special insight into the mind of God for you. Perhaps that person began by saying, "God told me to tell you . . ." If you feel comfortable, share that time with your study partners. Why are such claims dangerous?

22. Eliphaz wasn't the only friend to claim special knowledge. So did Bildad. After Job protested his innocence (although he never claimed he was sinless), Bildad pounced on Job. Read Job 8:1–4.

a. Bildad claims to know why Job's children died. He said they received punishment for their sin. He claims that their deaths proved they were sinful. Bildad seems to have a good point—and perhaps Job's heart jumped in fright. Why? For help refer back to Job 1:5.

b. However, something is very wrong about Bildad's accusation. Why is it incorrect to assume that tragedies come as a result of God's punishment for sin? For help, refer to Jesus' words in Luke 13:1–5 or John 9:1–3.

23. If Bildad is correct, we are all in trouble. All suffering, he says, is the result of God punishing our sin. But worse than that, he tells Job that he can come back to God only under certain conditions.

a. According to Bildad, what are those conditions? (See Job 8:5–6.) Why is Bildad so tragically wrong?

b. Bildad simply doesn't know the Gospel. And unless we know the Gospel, we, too, can fall prey to modern-day Bildads. What does Jesus say in Matthew 9:12–13 that completely reverses Bildad's words? If you suffered under the advice of a modern-day Bildad, how can Jesus' words give you hope and peace in the midst of suffering?

24. Eliphaz speaks dramatically about his visiting spirit, ghost, or phantom. We would expect that whatever secrets this spirit will reveal would be as dramatic as Eliphaz's buildup! But we are in for a disappointment. Reread Job 4:17.

a. Perhaps Eliphaz (or his ghost) thinks he is astute, but the "revelation" we hear from him is trite. What is the obvious answer to Eliphaz's question? Why do you think Eliphaz asked such a question?

b. Job never said he was perfectly "right . . . pure" before God. Why do you think Eliphaz put these words into Job's mouth?

25. Reread Job 4:18–19. Eliphaz is like many who think they are wise because they can so easily run down the human race. That isn't difficult, nor is it helpful for Job. Man is hopelessly bad because of his sinful nature. There is no sexism here, because the same is true of

woman. Romans 3:10–12 confirms this. Yet what is scripturally wrong with Eliphaz's humanity-bashing? And is our predicament truly hopeless, as Eliphaz implies? (For help see Genesis 9:6 and Romans 5:6–11.)

26. How does the birth of Jesus show that the views of Eliphaz are false and hollow? How does Jesus' birth give us hope where Eliphaz would tear us down?

In Closing

Encourage participants to begin the following activities:
- Pray together Mary's song, called the Magnificat, in Luke 1:46–55, which expresses her joy in how God restores His people to Himself. If you pray it together, be sure to use the same Bible versions.
- You may find the Magnificat in *Lutheran Worship*, pages 228–30, or *The Lutheran Hymnal*, page 43.
- Read Job 10–15 to prepare for the next lesson.

Close with prayer.

Lesson 3

Looking into Secret Sins
Part 2

Let the Buyer Beware

You've heard the old adage Let the buyer beware. That also goes for buying into advice, especially religious advice of well-meaning friends. Job's friends have begun to lay down the foundation of their case against Job. They will try to convince him that he is guilty of some secret sin and that his suffering is undeniable proof of his guilt.

But let the buyer beware! Advice should be examined and cross-examined. Not all religious advice is sound and healthy. Religious quacks may outnumber medical charlatans.

In the following exercise, you have the challenge to cross-examine the friends' advice. Remember, they are trying to prove that Job is guilty of secret sin. Your assignment is to see whether their presumptions are correct. Rely only on Scripture to judge.

Cross-Examining the Comforter

We will select Eliphaz as our sample comforter. Notice that he talks about justice and power (Law), never about the forgiveness of sins (Gospel). His line of thinking seems to go this way:

Step 1: WHEREAS God is almighty and His ways cannot be comprehended or understood by mere mortals "who dwell in houses of clay" (Job 4:19); and

Step 2: WHEREAS God is immeasurably higher than the angels whom He charges with error (v. 18);

Step 3: THEREFORE, God's justice is far beyond anything we can expect to understand (v. 21); and

Step 4: FURTHERMORE, we have no assurance that God forgives our sin and loves us regardless of our circumstances (no verses contain the Gospel);

Step 5: AND FINALLY, it is useless for sufferers to complain to God, because they must repent of their secret sins before God will even listen (5:1–2).

Notice that Step 5 applies only to Job and those who suffer! Eliphaz, remember, thinks he has special insider information when it comes to God, as we read in 4:12–17. Those who do not suffer apparently have access to the Divine Ear, according to Comforter Eliphaz.

If you are not already in your small groups, rejoin them. With your study partners, cross-examine the comforter's line of thinking. Your discussion leader can give you some pointers if you desire. You may use the following as discussion prompts:

27. Examine the statements in Steps 1 through 5. Which agree with Scripture? Which do not agree? Do they clarify Scripture or confuse it? Explain your answer.

28. Perhaps you've heard advice similar to Eliphaz's. How did you (or how would you) react to it? Would his advice help your faith in God's grace grow or not? Explain your answer.

"Show Me My Sin!"

In the suggested reading for this week, Job repeatedly protested that he was innocent, but his friends thought he was being too stubborn to confess. Judge for yourself by reading Job's own words in Job 6:24–25, 28–30.

29. Which is it: Is Job defiantly refusing to admit wrongdoing, and these words are just a bluff? Or is he sincerely wanting any correction that he might have coming? Give reasons for your answer.

30. The language of the Hebrew text shows that Job is asking for some straight talk from his friends. Why would he so boldly ask them to prove his secret sin?

31. Share a time when you may have asked the same question as Job. Why was it important to you to have someone show you your sin?

Zophar, perhaps the cruelest comforter, had to wait to speak his turn, but when he does he is full of cold rage. Read Job 11:1–6.

32. Zophar heard Job's, "Show me my sin," but he did not hear the man's pain. Rigid and aloof, Zophar can only believe that Job's suffering is caused by his sin. It isn't. But why can't Zophar see that? Share your views freely.

33. Read 11:2–12. Zophar defends God by insulting Job. He is enraged at Job's speeches and questions (vv. 2–4). God is too lofty (vv. 7–9) for a man like Job (v. 12). Why do you think Zophar took this approach instead of simply and directly answering Job's request to be shown his sin? How would you respond if a friend took this approach to you if you were suffering?

"How I Wish God Would Speak!"

Reread Job 11:1–6, and add verses 7–12.

You can easily see that Zophar is angry at Job. He wishes God would speak in condemnation of Job (vv. 5–6). Job wanted God to tell him He still loved him, but Zophar thought that if God spoke at all, it would only be to express His anger at Job. He does not think Job can claim to be pure in God's sight, forgiven by grace through faith (v. 4; see Ephesians 2:8–9). Zophar apparently does not understand the Gospel.

34. Zophar's cruelty comes through clearly. He tells Job, who is pushed to the farthest edge of human suffering, that Job is getting by with less suffering than he deserves (v. 6)!

a. But Zophar is putting words into God's mouth. From what you know of Scripture, how is Zophar misrepresenting God? For example, see Jeremiah 31:34.

b. If you were suffering, how would you react to Zophar's remarks?

35. Zophar strongly implies that God's silence toward Job is a sign of how disgustingly sinful Job is. Many who suffer are tempted to believe the same thing. But is that how God acts? Select one of the examples below of what God does when it comes to sin. Ask someone who is familiar with the incident to summarize.

David's sin with Bathsheba (2 Samuel 12:1–14)

God saves Noah and his family (Genesis 6:5–14, 17–18)

God confronts King Nebuchadnezzar with his sin of self-idolatry (Daniel 4:28–37)

Jesus interacts with the woman at the well (John 4:7–26, 39)

36. When Zophar spoke of God punishing Job less than he deserved, it still sounded threatening. Yet how does God "exacting less" sound to you?

37. How is it possible that God does not remember our sin? (For help, see Hebrews 8:1–13, especially v. 12.)

38. If God no longer remembers our sin because of Jesus' new covenant through His blood, then there is no reason for Him to give us the silent treatment or turn a cold shoulder or deaf ear to us. How can this be good news to someone suffering pain or loss?

In Closing

Encourage participants to begin the following activities:
- Read together Psalm 41 and John 13:18–19, considering how Job would hear and respond to these words.
- Read Job 16–21 to prepare for the next lesson.

Close with prayer.

Lesson 4

Suffering and Prayer

God and His Friends

There may be times in our lives when we think or feel that God treats us unfairly! What in the world do we do with those thoughts and feelings? How can we bring ourselves to pray to God when we think He's got something against us—especially when bad times hit?

In other words, how do we pray when we are suffering?

That's what we will explore in this session of our study of Job. Although Job did not always comprehend God and His ways, we will discover that God welcomes, even encourages, prayers with spunk.

Divide into small groups of three or four. Share what you think about praying at a time of suffering. You may use the discussion prompts below. After letting all participants share, reassemble into your large group.

39. If you were thrown into a pit of suffering, how would you pray? Do you think complaining to God is a proper form of prayer? Give reasons for your answer.

40. Suppose upon telling a friend about your suffering, your friend's advice was, "Smile, God loves you." How would you respond or react? Would you think your friend sympathizes with you? Why or why not?

Barriers to Prayer

You may have noticed that the further you read through the Book of Job, the more Job talks with God and the less he talks with his friends. But why didn't he start out that way? Why didn't he approach the Lord in prayer from the beginning? In other words, did Job find something getting in his way? Did he run into some barriers to prayer?

Read what was going through Job's mind in Job 9:1–4 (optional vv. 5–13) and 14–22. Here, Job is not talking to God. He is talking about God to his friends. He is explaining to them why he feels he cannot bring his cause to God.

41. Reread verses 3–4. Job imagines what would happen if we could bring God to court. Yet he realizes that even if God would permit that, we would not be able to answer one question in a thousand that He might hurl at us. Why not?

42. Job's friends offered him how-to formulas to get God to restore him. They said if Job would pray for mercy and forgiveness (for the secret sin), God would give him back everything he lost. But Job protests. He knows God's love is not conditional, not based on our actions, and not earned by our repentance. Why not? Why is the advice of the friends so absurd? (See vv. 3–14).

43. But there's another reason Job protests against his friends' advice. Job doesn't want mercy. He wants justice. He doesn't want forgiveness for some supposed sin. He wants vindication. By faith he knows God loves him, but he wants visible proof that his suffering is not punishment and that his friends' accusation is wrong.

a. The three friends, of course, think Job is being stubborn. They would tell him this attitude is his barrier to prayer and to God. On this point, would you agree with Job's friends? Give reasons for your answer.

b. Let's take that same question and slant it a different way: Suppose Job's friends are wrong, and Job is not simply being stubborn. Should he pray for forgiveness and mercy anyway? Is this what God wants out of Job? Why or why not?

44. Perhaps you have found yourself in a similar dilemma. Of course, none of us is sinless; but suppose we are suffering due to no fault of our own. Hoping that God will rescue us from our suffering, should we pray for forgiveness even though we don't know of any sin? Should we assume God is angry and punishing us? Why or why not? Take time to think about your answer. Mull it over, and jot some notes below. Share your thoughts with your study partners.

Call for a Referee

Still, something is apparently blocking Job from praying, at least at this stage. He can't argue with God and win. He can't trump up an artificial confession of fictitious sins. He can't control an all-powerful, all-wise God. He is perfectly helpless, and he knows it.

And that's it! Surprisingly (maybe even to Job), our helplessness is the very key to the problem of suffering.

Read Job 9:32–35. Here Job exposes the real problem. It's not just about pain itself. It's not just discovering why bad things happen. It's deeper than that. It's about God and us. What does God think about us and feel toward us, especially when we're hurting? That's the question!

Job believes he knows what God thinks of him! Unlike the friends, Job realizes that he cannot make himself righteous before God. Even if he would drop his complaint against God and try to clean himself (see Job 9:27–31), God would still consider him dirty, since he cannot remove his sin by his own efforts (9:14–15).

45. Earlier, Eliphaz tells Job that God uses His divine power to help Job (see Job 5:9–27). But Job sees no comfort in God's power

(9:10–20). Instead, what does Job fear when it comes to God's power (9:4, 12–20, 22–25)?

46. Read verse 33. So, Job needs someone who can settle the quarrel between God and Job. The Hebrew word for this person, *arbiter,* means "referee" or "umpire." This person is someone who can bring God and Job together by laying "his hand on us both" as a friend of both. Think of a referee in a wrestling match cautioning both wrestlers.

a. A referee would have to have as much power, authority, or strength as the strongest wrestler. Why? How could someone like this help Job?

b. Have you ever felt a need for a referee between you and God? Share what that time was like (only if you wish). How could someone like a referee help you?

47. It's one thing to wish for a referee between us and God; it's quite another thing to actually have one. On a board or newsprint flip chart, list some of the qualifications this referee would have to have. Whom do you know that meets these qualifications?

Just What You Asked For!

As soon as Job talks about needing a referee, he turns to Him. How can we be so sure? Closely read Job 10.

48. Job's complaints in this chapter are no different, but his audience is. How do you know he is not complaining to his friends any longer, but to God? (See v. 2.)

49. Only moments before, Job declared he could not talk with God unless some changes were made (9:33–35). What had to change before Job could talk to God without fear? What has to change before we can talk to God without fear?

50. Job truly believed that God was punishing him, so he needed someone to "take His rod away from me" (9:34–35). How did our referee, Jesus, remove God's rod not only from Job, but from us too? For help, see Isaiah 52:13–53:12 and Galatians 3:13.

How Open with God?

After suffering the loss of all his wealth, the deaths of his children, the scorn of his wife, as well as his disease or illness, Job honestly thought that God was against him. As we saw, initially he couldn't even talk directly to God. And then, while pleading for a referee between God and himself, Job realized he could talk, or pray, to God after all. He could air his case, wrestle with God, take God on. Why?

It is not because Job thinks he can handle God on his own. Rather, it is because Job does have an arbiter, a referee, a mediator. Job has a God-for-him who can take on God's wrath. This is Jesus Christ.

Job is not alone in this. We have Jesus, God's only-begotten Son, who is also God Himself.

51. Skim through Job 10 again. On a scale of 1 to 10 (1 being very closed, 10 being extremely open), how open with God was Job?

Would you feel comfortable complaining (or lamenting) to God as Job did? Why or why not?

52. Read Hebrews 4:14–16. High priests are go-betweens between us and God. Why is Jesus the ultimate High Priest?

53. The text implies that Jesus sympathizes with us. Literally, the Greek root behind *sympathize* means "to suffer with." God doesn't sit on a throne, zapping us with punishments. Instead, in Christ, He joins us, suffers with us, and one day will free us from all suffering. How can this good news change the way you believe, think, and feel about God?

54. Reread verse 16. So then, how can we approach God's throne of grace? In light of this promise, how might your prayers change? What topics of conversation may you now boldly share with your heavenly Father?

In Closing

Encourage participants to begin the following activities:
- Take a few moments to list some new and bold petitions that you may take to God's throne of grace. How can your church comfort the suffering and reach out to the dying? What needs do the sufferers in your group have that you can take to your heavenly Father's throne?
- Read Job 22–25 to prepare for the next lesson.

Close with prayer.

Lesson 5

Christ to the Rescue

The Will of God?

Ask a volunteer to read the following:

"Everything that happens is the will of God." That's what most Dutch schoolchildren were once taught, and that's what Cornelis firmly believed. And he thought that was just fine until, one day, Germany overran and occupied his country. And even though Cornelis didn't think that God actually drove the Panzer tanks, flew the Messerschmidts, or dropped the bombs on Rotterdam, he did believe that it must have been the will of God because "Everything that happens is the will of God."

Ever since that evil day, Cornelis was known to say: "Let God sit on His high and mighty throne. But then let God leave me completely alone! We're better off without Him."

Discuss Cornelis's situation.

55. Cornelis believes that everything that happens is the will of God. How would you respond to him?

56. Job also believes that everything that happens is the will of God, even pain and suffering (Job 6:4; 16:11–14.). Yet, unlike Cornelis, Job never abandons God. What do you think caused the difference?

For Me? Or against Me?

We can never know with certainty why one person trusts in God while another does not. But Cornelis only saw God as against him. And if you think God is against you, it is very difficult to trust Him! Job, too, felt that God was against him. Read 16:9, 12–13.

Yet, at the same time, Job also believed God loved him and forgave him. Although Job's thinking about God can be very confused and confusing, and although he can even grow angry at God (ch. 24), part of Job always knows that God is on his side. While God seems to be against Job, He is also for him.

57. In the last session, we saw that Job had a referee between him and God. How does having a referee or mediator between God and man help us? (See also Job 9:32–35.)

58. Job's friends again told him that if he was a godly and faithful believer, he simply wouldn't be in this terrible situation (Job 15). Then Job lost his temper! He sounds angrier than ever at the comforters and at God. Read Job 16:1–17. (In v. 1–6, Job is speaking to his friends; in v. 7–17, he is speaking to God.) List three charges Job makes against God.

59. Job's frustration is due to the fact that he knows God better than that. He knows that God isn't the kind of God who wills evil on His children. So how can God now attack him like this? Of course, not knowing the satanic source of his suffering, Job hurls these charges at God Himself. The reader knows that Satan actually brought about Job's suffering, but God still allowed it.

a. Do you think Job sinned by charging God with these crimes? Share and explain your answer. Listen to the views of others. (For help, see Job 40:3–8; 42:3–6.)

b. Did you ever see God in the same way that Job does here? Share what that was like (only if you wish). What finally helped you through that situation? or are you not through it yet?

60. Now read Job 16:18. Job doesn't think he will see justice in this life. Unlike his friends, however, he has a sure hope that he will see justice eventually, and his blood will cry out for it.

a. Perhaps this text reminds you of another person's blood crying out for justice. If so, who? (See Genesis 4:8–10.)

b. Notice how God responded to the cry in the Genesis 4 text. Do you think God always takes such special notice of the suffering cries of all His people, or are there times when God seems deaf to people's cries? Share your answers with others.

"My Witness"

At the very time when Job seems angriest at God, he gives one of the strongest confessions of faith in God, his witness. Read Job 16:19–21.

61. Besides calling Him "witness," Job mentions several other actions of God. List them below.

62. Which work of the Witness best fills the title or description below? Share with one another the reasons why you chose the title you did.

a. "I approach the Judge of the universe to show Him My perfectly obedient life which fulfilled His Law. That is one reason I am called the . . ."

b. "I use My high position with God to speak for you. That is one reason I am called the . . ."

c. "I hear your weeping, and I plead for you to My Father. That is one reason I am called the . . ."

d. "I do all this for you, not as a paid attorney might, but I do it all because I am your . . ."

63. Verse 21 gives us a big clue as to who this witness is, and why He is so effective. Review with one another why this witness can only be Jesus Christ.

Read Hebrews 2:14–18. List several reasons why Jesus, being both God and man, is the most effective intercessor we could have.

a. Verse 14: by sharing our flesh and blood, when Jesus died, He destroyed . . .

b. Verse 16: Jesus doesn't help the angels, but He helps . . .

c. Verse 17: God's Son was made like us in every way, except sin. As a result, God the Father has a faithful High Priest, and we have . . .

d. Verse 18: because Jesus, fully a man, suffered, that means that when we suffer . . .

64. Jesus pleads for us with His Father. Jesus and His Father are not separate or rival gods! They (with the Spirit) are the one triune God. Knowing that, what do you think the response of God the Father will be when His Son pleads for us? How might this change the way you pray? or how you see God acting toward you?

Which Throne!

We talk about when God took on human flesh as the incarnation. You can read about the incarnation in Matthew 1:18–25 and Luke

1:26–38. Today we will read about it in John 1:1–18, where Jesus is called the Word.

65. "The Word became flesh and tented awhile among us" is a very literal translation of verse 14. The "tent" alludes to the tabernacle and temple in the Old Testament, where God dwelt among His people to bless them. The people saw God's glory as He lived in their midst. How does the Word still live among us today? (See Matthew 18:20; 28:20.)

66. In the opening scenario, Cornelis said, "Let God sit on His high and mighty throne." The Dutchman could only see a sovereign God commanding everything from His throne in heaven. What is correct about Cornelis's view? What is incorrect?

67. Perhaps Cornelis was looking at the wrong throne. We best see what God is like when we see Jesus. The best view of how God thinks about and feels toward us is from the foot of the cross at Calvary.

a. What do you see about God there: a God who is for you or against you? How can this help you when you feel that God has abandoned you or is punishing you?

b. How can you help other sufferers with this view of God?

In Closing

Encourage participants to begin the following activities:
- God became man in Jesus Christ. God Himself, therefore, walked around in human flesh and blood to live among us, sympathize with us, and save us. Select a favorite Christmas or Advent hymn that picks up on this theme for your closing prayer.
- Read Job 26–31 to prepare for the next lesson.

Close with prayer.

Lesson 6

With Friends like These

The Case of Charr and Karen

Ask a volunteer to read the following scenario:

Charr was smoldering and not hiding it well. She dug her nails deeper into the arm of the chair, clawing horseshoe-shaped scars into the leather.

"Would you like to say that again?" she asked, her words sizzling. The woman on the other side of the desk sighed condescendingly. Obviously she had heard denials like Charr's before and didn't believe them.

"All I'm saying," said the woman, "is that in the eight years I've been a staff counselor in this church, I've run into dozens of cases just like yours, Charr. And in most, the woman involved was not completely innocent. I'm just asking you to be honest with yourself."

"What are you implying?" said Charr, livid now. "For crying out loud, Karen. I was raped! Nobody asks for that!"

Karen sighed again and tapped her pen on the glass surface of her desk, trying to look as professional as she could. "This is going to take longer than either of us want, Charr, if you're going to insist on your innocence. If you want healing, then you're going to have to come clean." She folded her arms, stared at Charr, and waited.

For what seemed like hours, she sat openmouthed, looking at her friend, her counselor, her spiritual mentor in total disbelief. To say she was surprised didn't begin to cover it. Charr felt betrayed.

"Well," Karen began, propping her elbows on the desk and replacing her reading glasses, "if you're not going to say anything, then I really don't know how I can help you. And, for that matter, I don't know how God can help you either."

"God?" Charr blurted out. "How can you talk about God like that? I've been victimized, and God can't help me?"

"Look, Charr." Karen's voice changed slightly, becoming as kind as she could make it. "Everything turns out for good. That's what the Bible says. And even though you refuse to see your own responsibility in this for now, eventually you'll repent. And God can turn this whole thing into good."

"I don't think you're listening to me, Karen," Charr said, wiping away tears.

"I'm hearing you, Charr," Karen said in a correcting tone. "But now it's time for you to hear me. God must have let this happen to teach you something. Suffering is good for us, Charr. It can bring us closer to God. Trust Him."

At that, Charr rose out of the leather chair. She thrust her tissues into her purse and closed it with a resounding snap.

"Where are you going?" Karen asked.

Charr didn't answer until she reached the door. "Trust God?" she asked acidly. "Not your God, Karen. It's obvious that your God has never been hurt."

The above scenario is fictional, but similar dramas have been acted out many times with well-meaning counselors. In some Christian circles, the standard reaction to suffering, tragedy, and even death is to advise, "It must be God's will. Confess your sins and accept it." As the saying goes, "With friends like these, who needs enemies?" Job certainly must have thought the same thing about his friends.

The Charr/Karen scenario contains bits and pieces of the same advice and counsel that Eliphaz, Bildad, and Zophar gave to Job. Discuss Karen's advice to Charr. You may use the discussion prompts below.

68. Briefly share your overall impression of Charr, then of Karen. Would you want to return to Karen as your counselor?

69. Karen thought she understood Charr thoroughly. What shows that she may have listened to Charr but didn't really hear or understand her?

70. List at least two or three points where you think Karen's assumptions are off base. These may be assumptions about Charr, about being a victim, or about God and Scripture.

71. Charr felt betrayed because Karen, a sister in Christ and a woman herself, condemned her instead of supporting her. Why is it so vitally important that in times of crisis your friends trust and believe in you?

72. At the end of the scenario, Charr walked out with a bitter comment. Do you think Charr was talking about the true God or about Karen's view of God? Explain your answer.

When It's Not "Gospel Truth"

When we read the Book of Job, one of the first things we have to get out of our heads is that every word of Job is "Gospel truth." Rather, in the Book of Job, God also allows us to look at some common (and tragic) errors in religious thinking, which, in the end, take our eyes away from the Gospel.

Not only did Job's friends mislead him by their words, they also misled him by their attitude and actions. They claimed to speak and act on God's behalf. The truth is that they sounded and acted more like messengers of the Accuser himself, Satan.

A. "God Won't Help, Unless . . ."

In the Charr/Karen scenario, Karen virtually tells Charr that God's help is conditional, that God won't help unless Charr first repents. There is just enough truth here to make the lie believable. Certainly, God calls for repentance when we sin. But Karen incorrectly

51

assumes that Charr sinned and refuses to repent. Job's friends say the same thing. Read Eliphaz's words in Job 5:1.

73. According to Eliphaz, can Job expect God to answer his prayers for help? Why or why not?

74. Has anyone ever told you that God was abandoning you because you did not meet His conditions? If so, share (only if you wish).

75. One blatant error that lies behind this bad advice is what we call works-righteousness. It means that our works, even our repentance, can somehow win God's favor. However, when we need to repent, what is it that motivates us? (See Romans 2:4.)

76. Friends like Eliphaz assume that when we suffer, God is giving us the silent treatment; therefore, it's useless for Job to call out to God. How would you respond to that claim? (For help, see Jeremiah 33:3 and Psalm 50:15.)

77. Job's suffering eased tremendously when he finally realized that God had never abandoned him. From your own experience, share how this can happen. How can true friends reflect God's presence to the suffering person?

B. "You're Not Hearing Me!"

One of the greatest hurts the friends inflicted on Job was listening to his words but not hearing what he was saying. They would put words into Job's mouth that he never said (see Bildad's remark in Job 8:6), then blast him for it. Their impatience with Job blocked their ears. Suffering people need friends with broad shoulders and open ears.

Read Job's expectations of his friends in Job 6:12–14.

78. Eliphaz told Job, "Hang in there; it'll get better." But why can't Job hold out any longer (v. 12)? If you were suffering, how would a "Hang in there" make you feel?

79. Job is not saying that he abandoned God, but that he would need friends around even if he did. Why is it especially vital for friends to persevere when the suffering person seems to be losing faith?

80. Sometimes we need to hear the hurt more than the actual words. Job's friends, quite to the contrary, heard his words and read in their own thoughts. They gave pat answers to questions he did not ask, and they did not answer the questions he did ask. How can we avoid doing the same? (See Proverbs 17:17.)

81. We have a powerful promise from God: God hears beyond our words and understands our unspoken hurts! Read Romans 8:15–16, 26–27. Share how this promise can help when you wonder if God really understands your hurts.

C. "You're Preaching at Me!"

If a husband is truly loving, he will never tell his wife as she gives birth, "I know what you're going through." Unless we walk a mile in the other person's shoes, we cannot truly sympathize with him or her.

That principle didn't stop Job's friends, however. We all have had friends who lectured, not listened, and who pointed fingers at our face instead of putting their arm around our shoulder.

Read how Job felt about being preached at in Job 16:1–4.

82. Job is probably responding to Eliphaz's pompous speech in Job 15:1–35. Why do you think he called his friends "miserable comforters" (16:2)?

A young pastor and his wife were suffering from attacks of gossip in their parish. When a neighboring pastor came to counsel them, he admonished them for not trusting God's promises, then recited three Scripture texts. The young woman replied, "Stop shooting me with Bible passages!"

83. Reread Eliphaz's sermon in Job 15:11. Apparently, "the comforts of God" did not come across as very comforting to Job. Why doesn't reciting Bible texts always help the hurting person? What's missing?

84. Reread Job 16:4. Job's remarks drip with sarcasm. Why is it easy for his friends to preach to him? What strong warning does this give us when we try to help a suffering friend?

D. "But It's Good for You!"

Perhaps when you were children your parents forced some bitter-tasting medicine into your mouth, adding, "But it's good for you." You probably didn't believe it then. You may still have doubts about it now.

Dr. Martin Luther spent a lifetime rescuing God's people from the wretched myth that our suffering is good for us because it somehow increases our favor with God. Strangely, however, that belief still lingers when we fail to separate the fact from the myth. The fact is that God does use suffering to bring about good for us. But that doesn't mean that our suffering, in and of itself, is good.

There's a big difference between the fact and the myth. But it's one that Job's comforters (and their modern-day counterparts) fail to see.

85. Read Eliphaz's words in Job 5:17–18. There is a ring of truth to this speech. Compare his words with Hebrews 12:5–11.

a. In the Middle Ages, the illegitimate children of royalty were not disciplined and were allowed to do whatever they pleased. However, they also had no share in the king's inheritance. Kings would discipline their legitimate heirs severely, if necessary, and train them well. Why? Since we are God's royal children and heirs of Christ, how can this help us accept discipline?

b. Although Eliphaz's words are similar to what Hebrews says, what is obviously missing: the very thing that could offer us hope?

86. Reread verse 18. According to Eliphaz, God both wounds and binds, shatters and heals. From what you know of Scripture, is Eliphaz correct or not? Give reasons for your answer.

87. Under Christ-controlled conditions, yes, suffering can set off a chain of events that helps us grow as God's children. But suffering itself cannot do that. What does? (See Romans 5:3–5.)

Job's Bigger God

What we need when we're suffering (and what our friends need) is a much bigger picture of God than offered by Job's three friends. With utter disgust and bitter sarcasm, Job finally dismisses them, implying that their advice is from Satan, not God (Job 26:4).

Although it means jumping to the end of the story, read what God finally has to say about the three friends in Job 42:7–9.

The three friends are condemned; Job is vindicated. In their endless tirades against Job, none of them ever even hinted that they, too, need to live under the grace, mercy, and forgiveness of God.

88. What reason does God give for His anger at the three friends? What caution should this give to those who want to speak for God?

89. Although they stand condemned, God does not give the three friends the same treatment they gave Job. What does He do instead?

My Redeemer Lives

We know now, since we peeked ahead to the end of the story, that Job is vindicated. But all along, Job had clung to the hope that God would come to his rescue.

Let's briefly look at a text that we will treat more deeply in a later session. Read Job's best-known statement of faith in Job 19:23–27.

90. There is no doubt in Job's mind that this Redeemer (or Vindicator) is his Arbiter, his Friend. It is Jesus Christ, the Son of God. Job knows that even if his present suffering kills him, his Redeemer will still rescue him. Does Job believe he has eternal life? Why do you think this passage inspired the hymn "I Know that My Redeemer Lives"?

91. Jesus rescues us from God's righteous indignation by putting Himself between us and God's wrath. Since Jesus suffered all God's wrath on the cross in our place, what is God's disposition toward us now? (See Romans 8:1.) Why is this vitally important to remember, especially when we are suffering?

92. Earlier, we heard Job's expectations of his friends. Even if the suffering person seems to be forsaking God, a friend will remain devoted to him (Job 6:14). Share how Jesus fulfills Job's expectation in Matthew 9:35–36

Romans 5:6–8

2 Timothy 2:13

93. Share a time when these texts, describing the devotion of Christ Jesus to you, helped or could help you, either when you suffer or are comforting the suffering.

In Closing

Encourage participants to begin the following activities:
- In your daily prayers, include members of your congregation who are suffering and despairing of God's help.
- Read Job 32–37 to prepare for the next lesson.

Close with prayer.

Lesson 7

Where Is God
When I Need Him?

Changing Players

As you have been following the suggested readings ("In Closing") at the end of each session, you may have come to the same conclusion that many Bible commentators have: The arguments between Job and the three friends just go on and on, round and round. Often they seem to repeat themselves and talk past each other.

Don't feel bad if their arguments wearied you! The fact is that Job and the three friends are themselves weary—bone weary of the whole business. For us, that is good to know. It shows that Job is very much like us. Who among us doesn't also grow weary of both the suffering that never seems to go away and the seemingly endless wrestling with God over our suffering?

In today's session we'll see another friend enter the scene. He is Elihu, a young man who has been sitting and listening to Job and the three friends all along. When the others reach a stalemate, Elihu finally speaks.

Read Job 32:1–22.

94. Elihu feels he has been patiently listening long enough. If he doesn't speak now, he will burst (v. 19).

a. From reading this chapter, how would you describe Elihu? Is he respectful and caring, or arrogant and brash?

b. From what you know so far of Elihu, what kind of comforter do you think he will be for Job? Explain.

95. Reread verse 12. Elihu is correct. Toward the end of their arguments, the three other friends make ridiculous accusations against Job. (See Eliphaz's tirade in Job 22:6–11.) Yet not one accusation could be proved. Why is it good that Elihu cleared the air on this point?

96. But Elihu does have an accusation against Job. See Job 33:8–12.

a. Do you think Elihu's charge is accurate or not? Give reasons for your answer.

b. Often suffering people today feel that God is against them, that He is their enemy. Elihu believed that this was a sin that must be quickly corrected. How would you respond to a believing friend who thought God was his or her enemy?

97. As strongly as Elihu believes that he is wiser than the other friends of Job, he eventually argues, as they did, that suffering is a way God speaks (or reveals Himself) to us. Read Job 33:14–18.

98. Elihu sounds much like Eliphaz (see 4:12–17). But he differs radically in his view of why God allows suffering. According to Elihu, what is God trying to prevent by permitting suffering (33:18)?

Why Does Job Resist?

As true as Elihu's words sound, a fatal flaw lies behind them. People may certainly suffer for the wrong they do. A thief is arrested and jailed. An adulterer suffers a divorce. Certainly, God may use that kind of suffering to turn an unrepentant person from sin.

But suffering is not God's only way of speaking to us! If it were, Eliphaz, Bildad, and Zophar would be right, and Job would be wrong. Then we would know God only as the God of Law, the God who condemns our sin. We would never know that He is also the God of the Gospel, who forgives our sins and grants us life eternal through Jesus.

Job resisted because he knew God better than any of the friends. So Job stubbornly held on to his belief that God is also a God of grace and mercy. When Job cried, "Oh, that I knew where I might find Him, that I might come even to His seat!" (Job 23:3), he was looking for the Redeemer, the Savior, the God we can find only in the Gospel.

99. God's Law, His power and condemnation of sin, is revealed in creation and in our consciences, as well as in Scripture. But God reveals His Gospel, His grace and forgiveness, only through Christ in His Word and Sacraments. Why is this vitally important to remember, especially in times of suffering? In other words, what kind of God might we find if we look someplace other than the Word and Sacraments?

100. Scripture is God's written Word to us. The Word reveals to us both the Law and the Gospel. While the Law shows us our sin and need for a Savior, only the Gospel shows us our Savior from sin and the mediator between God and us, Jesus Christ.

a. Unlike the other friends, Elihu wasn't completely off base! What strong Gospel message does Elihu share with Job (and us) in Job 33:22–28? What does our mediator, Jesus, do for Job and for us?

b. Our mediator tells God the Father that in order to rescue us, "I have found a ransom." A ransom is the payment given to buy back someone who already belongs to you. What ransom was found (Matthew 20:28)?

101. Job would grow to understand that God never abandons those He ransoms and rescues from the pit! Instead, what does Christ do? (See Job 33:25–26.)

102. Job had difficulty seeing through his suffering to a gracious God. His experience with God clashed with what he knew about God. So, to him, God was hidden (Job 23:3). Share what you might have said to Job (or a suffering friend) that is different from what Elihu said.

Finally, God Revealed!

Job gets what he has asked for. Interestingly, Job never asked God to restore his property, wealth, or children. He just asked to meet with God.

Finally, God answers his prayer! He comes to Job. And although God has some strong words to say, overall, God's talk with Job is full of grace and love.

103. Read Job 38:1. God spoke to Job out of a whirlwind. This is precisely what Job was afraid of (see Job 9:17). Why? (Job 1:19 might show us why!) But what happened that completely surprised Job when God spoke from the whirlwind?

104. Read Job 38:2–3. This may be God's strongest word against Job. He said that Job spoke about Him in ignorance, accusing Him of being unjust and angry. How will God solve Job's lack of knowledge? Today, how do we come to know God and what He is like?

105. In verse 3 God offers to speak to Job as though the two of them were equals—man to man, so to speak. His purpose is to instruct and build up Job, not put him down. How do you think Job felt about this invitation? How would you? Does God make the same offer to us today? (See Isaiah 1:18.)

Letting God Do the Talking

Throughout the next several chapters (38–41), God does most of the talking, and Job listens (except for Job's "repentance" in 40:3–5.) If you look for specific answers to Job's questions, "Why is this happening to me?" "What sin have I committed?" etc., you won't find any. Some people find this extremely discouraging. They think God is evading Job and his questions, and, thus, evading ours.

106. But God is not evading anyone's questions. In fact, by not answering Job's question, "What sin have I committed to deserve this?" (as in Job 6:24), what is God saying to Job? to Job's friends? to us?

107. Job knew, of course, that all of us are sinful and deserve punishment in both this life and the next. But Job trusted that his gracious God would forgive him through his Arbiter, his Redeemer. Since he thought (incorrectly) that his suffering was punishment, he could not understand why God allowed it (Job 7:21). Therefore, Job accused God of being capricious, of not living up to His own divine standard of justice (9:22–24).

a. God showed Job how just and gracious He is. Read Job 40:8–14. What does God say to us when we're tempted to think we could run the universe more justly than He does? What is God's purpose in governing the universe?

b. Often we're tempted to wish we could take justice into our own hands, especially when neither God nor His servant, the government (Romans 13), seem to act quickly or harshly enough. Here, God is asking us to reexamine that desire: What might we do if we had God's power?

"Relax, I Am in Control"

The rest of God's speech to Job is a source of great comfort. Basically, God is telling Job and us that although there are forces of evil in the world beyond our control, He has everything well in hand. Nothing is beyond His control, and He controls all powers and forces for our eternal good.

108. Read Job 40:15–24. God asks Job to look at Behemoth. The Hebrew name means "Beasts" or "Beastliness." Many commentators and Bible footnotes suggest that Behemoth was a large land animal, possibly a hippopotamus, an elephant, or even a grass-eating dinosaur. However, here "Behemoth" is used as a proper name. He was one of the first of God's creations (v. 19), but now God approaches him with a sword.

64

Behemoth stands for the angel that rebelled against God—Satan—and all his hellish legions. That is why God slays him with His sword. What strong comfort can this passage bring you, especially when you feel vulnerable to the forces of pain and evil?

109. Throughout chapter 41 God speaks about Leviathan. Again, many commentators and Bible footnotes suggest an animal, possibly a crocodile or a flesh-eating dinosaur. Yet, as in the case of Behemoth, "Leviathan" is a proper name. Its description is similar to the dragon mentioned in Revelation 12:1–6. (See Job 41:20–21.) Leviathan apparently is an evil supernatural creature. God also promises to slay Leviathan with His sword (Isaiah 27:1). Read Job 41:33–34.

a. The words may sound familiar. What famous hymn by Martin Luther uses these words?

b. Who is Luther describing with these words?

110. No king or government (v. 34) or weapon has any power over Leviathan (vv. 26–29). Why is God reminding Job and us that by ourselves we humans have absolutely no power to overcome the satanic forces of evil in our world? Is God trying to frighten us, or is there a different reason? Give reasons for your answer. How did God slay Satan with His sword?

111. Although we do not, God has absolute power over all the forces of evil. They even become instruments in God's hands, so that

He can accomplish His saving mission. He will work it out for our good. How do these words from God compare to Romans 8:28?

112. Does God imply that there is a connection between the suffering of Job—and all believers—and Christ's suffering, by which He slew Leviathan? What is that connection? Read Matthew 16:21–28.

What Job Got

God never gave Job a direct answer to "Why am I suffering?" He only tells Job that He, God, is in control and that it will all come out for good. God is destroying evil in order to save us. God's promise was enough for Job. And Job was content.

Job didn't really get a precise answer, but he did get God. He got the Redeemer and Arbiter that he so terribly wanted. Job got a glimpse of how God, in Christ, would answer the problem of human suffering by becoming a human and suffering Himself. We have a much fuller view of how God did that in the New Testament through the suffering, death, and resurrection of Jesus Christ. We know that suffering is not a disgrace. It is not a sign that God has abandoned us. God's own Son suffered just to save you. And He was glad to do it!

Read Hebrews 12:2.

Christ Jesus could endure His suffering on account of the "joy that was set before Him." By His grace, you will share His glorious heavenly joy for eternity with Him in His kingdom. Share how that message can help you when you are suffering.

In Closing

Encourage participants to begin the following activities:
• Recite Psalm 70 responsively.
• Read Job 38–42 to prepare for the next lesson.

Close with prayer.

Lesson 8

The Lord Is Coming!

All's Well That Ends Well?

Believe it or not, some readers of Job are unhappy with its ending. They say it's too much like a fairy tale where everyone lived happily ever after. But that's only the milder criticism.

The stronger criticism about Job's happy ending is this: Since God blessed Job in the end, it may appear that Satan won the bet and Job believed in God only so he would be blessed. Let's see if these critics have a point. Review how Job's suffering began by reading Job 1:8–12.

The real issue is whether Job's (and our!) relationship to God is based on Law or Gospel. If it's Law, then God accepts and blesses us because we obediently do good works that please Him. If it's Gospel, then God accepts and blesses us simply because He loves us in Jesus Christ. If it's Law, then we earn our way to God. If it's Gospel, Jesus paid our way to God. If it's Law, then we serve God only so we will receive good things in life. If it's Gospel, we serve God out of love for our Savior, regardless of our circumstances in life.

113. Read verse 9. Satan thinks that Job is obedient and serves God for what reason?

114. What does Satan think Job will do if God stops giving Job so much? If Satan was correct, what would that say about Job's relationship with God?

Now read about God restoring Job in 42:10–16. Note the number of sheep, camels, oxen, and donkeys Job had at the beginning (1:3) and how many he had at his restoration (42:12).

115. Do you think the critics are correct? Does the ending of Job mean that believers are always blessed during this life? Did Job earn or deserve his restoration? Did Satan win the bet? Would Job have been a better hero had he gone to his grave faithful but poor? Give reasons for your answer.

116. Job needed to repent, but not for the reasons his friends gave. Job needed to repent because he thought God was unjust by letting an innocent man suffer. Job had questioned God's justice and mercy. Read Job 42:1–3.

a. Is there any hint here that Job confessed in order to be restored to his health and wealth? Explain your answer.

b. When was Job's health and wealth restored (v. 10)? Why do you think God finally restored Job, and even gave him twice what he previously had?

117. What was more important to Job than having his property and health returned to him? Give scriptural support for your answer.

Job and Us

Of course, this says something about our relationship to God too. The great twentieth-century Christian writer C. S. Lewis said, "The man who has everything and Christ has no more than the man who has just Christ."

118. In our Bible study group, we would all say this is true. But is it? Do we ever feel that God blesses some more than He blesses others, that He gives abundantly to some believers, but withholds from others? Why is it easy to envy fellow Christians whose lives seem to run smoothly when ours do not? Share a time when you thought or felt that way.

119. If we have ever felt envious in the way described above, we've probably fallen for the propaganda of Job's friends and believed that we can measure God's love for us on the basis of what He gives (or doesn't give). We're back in a Law-only relationship with Him.

a. Why would receiving the Sacrament of Holy Communion (Eucharist) be precisely what we need at those times? What does God give us in the Eucharist that can remove all doubts about His love for us?

b. Why can't Jesus Christ give us anything better than what He gives in this Sacrament? How does that make you feel when you commune?

c. Finally, how can Christ's sacramental gift overcome our envy of others? Do they have anything of real importance that we do not?

"How Long, O Lord?"

There is one big difference between Job and us. We know the end of his story. We do not know the end of ours. He was restored publicly. Perhaps the first people to see God restoring Job were Job's friends (Job 42:10).

One reason why God restored Job before he died, and why Job's vindication did not take place only in the next life, was so that the friends, and we, would firmly believe that God never abandons us. God stays with those He loves, even if outward circumstances seem to say otherwise.

But what about our story? If the present chapter of our life's story is full of hurts and suffering, what can we do? Let's start with a text we studied a few sessions back, Job 19:25–27.

120. Job proclaimed these words during one of his worst times of suffering. It seems he is almost ready to give up all hope in God. Yet he clings to one promise. Even if he loses life itself, what will he still have?

121. Our God loves physical things. He created the physical world. He Himself became a physical man. He gives us grace through physical sacraments. How do we know that our resurrection will also be physical?

122. Job's waiting for justice is not an isolated case. The entire Old Testament is a story of God's people waiting for God to rescue them. Read Habakkuk 1:1–4. Share a time when you may have thought or felt like Habakkuk.

123. Habakkuk, as well as Job, did not want something other than God. He wanted God. He knew that once we have God, we get everything else thrown in for good measure (Matthew 6:33).

a. Why are we sometimes tempted to want God for the things He can give us, rather than to want God for Himself? Does this ever happen in our relationships with others? with our children? with our spouse? with our parents? with friends at church?

b. How does God help us want Him only—and not simply because of the gifts He gives? (See 1 John 4:10 for a big hint.)

While We Wait

Who won? God did! God didn't bribe Job, and He doesn't bribe you either. He doesn't pay you off to stay faithful.

Think of it! You are here, gathered with His people, around His Word. Like Job, you, too, are proving Satan wrong by believing in and living in God's grace.

That God won is clear, because you are here despite your sufferings, past or present; your sins, past or present; your doubts, past or present; your fears, past or present. In other words, despite any circumstance in your life right now, God has gathered you with His people to wait for His return.

Read what waiting Christians are like in 2 Corinthians 4. Be sure to read yourself into this text.

124. To the unbelieving world, God is hidden. They cannot see Him in action, but we can. Where is God hidden, and why can't the unbelieving world see Him? (See vv. 3–4.)

125. On the outside, we may be battered around by doubts, sin, and suffering. But what is going on inside us? (See vv. 7–12.)

126. Read verses 13–18. List several ways we help one another to see God and His love for us.

127. God "hid" Himself in a real baby, and the unbelieving world didn't know that Mary's baby was also God's Son. God "hides" today in His Word, in the water of Baptism, and in the bread and wine of the Lord's Supper. How can "visiting" Jesus—by going where the Word and Sacraments are found—help you while you wait for His return?

128. Read 2 Corinthians 5:1–7. What characteristics of the waiting Christian describe you too?

"I'm Coming!"

Christians live the "hidden" life. That doesn't mean we hide our Christian faith. It means we live by faith in Jesus Christ. His love for us may not be visible in our circumstances; it is hidden in Christ, who comes to us in His Word and Sacraments.

Another word Christians sometimes use to describe how we wait is *eschatologically* (es-ka-to-loj-i-kal-lee). It means that since we know Jesus will come back, we look at things now from that point of view. It's like knowing the end of a book or movie and going through it with the ending in mind. It means that thanks to Jesus we know the end of our story! We will be with Jesus, face-to-face, and in the flesh.

Let's take an eschatological look into heaven to see what the end of our story is like. Read Revelation 21:1–5.

129. Why is the church (us) pictured as a bride and Jesus as the Bridegroom? What is this picture-language meant to express about us and Christ Jesus?

130. We will get what we long for, and God will get what He longs for. What is that? How can it help you now to know this will happen then?

131. Reread verse 4 and Jesus' last words in the Bible (Revelation 22:12–16, 20). What in this promise gives you comfort and strength now?

Living Eschatologically!

There is one clue that Job lived eschatologically, as a waiting Christian, even after God restored his wealth and health. You noticed that God doubled everything Job lost. At the end, Job had twice the number of sheep, oxen, camels, and donkeys as he did in the beginning.

132. Why do you think that Job did NOT receive twice the number of children? What comforting message does this offer you, especially if you have lost loved ones?

In Closing

Encourage participants to begin the following activities:
- Spend a few moments sharing with one another what you have appreciated about one another as you studied the Book of Job together. What new things have you discovered about God and His love for us in the Book of Job?
- As a closing hymn, sing "I Know that My Redeemer Lives" (*LW* 264, *TLH* 200). And sing it eschatologically!
"Lord Jesus, come quickly!"
"Yes, I am coming soon!"

Close with prayer.

Leader Notes

This guide is provided as a "safety net," a place to turn for help in answering questions and for enriching discussion. It will not answer every question raised in your class. Please read it, along with the questions, before class. Consult it in class only after exploring the Bible references and discussing what they teach. Please note the different abilities of your class members. Some will easily find the Bible passages listed in this study; others will struggle. To make participation easier, team up members of the class. For example, if a question asks you to look up several passages, assign one passage to one group, the second to another, and so on. Divide the work! Let participants present the answers they discover.

Preparing to Teach Job

To prepare to lead this study, read through the Book of Job. You might secure and read over a good commentary on the book or read the introduction to Job in the *Concordia Self-Study Bible* or a Bible handbook. Several maps of the Old Testament world at about 2000–1000 B.C. would also help, especially with the first three lessons.

The material in these notes is designed to help you in leading others through this portion of the Holy Scriptures. Nevertheless, this booklet is to be an aid to and not a substitute for your own study of and preparation for teaching the Book of Job.

If you have the opportunity, you will find it helpful to make use of other biblical reference works in the course of your study. The following are helpful commentaries: Rudolph E. Honsey, *Job,* People's Bible Commentary, (St. Louis: CPH, 1993); and John E. Hartley, *The Book of Job* (Grand Rapids: Eerdman's, 1988). Although it is not strictly a commentary, the section on Job in *The Word Becoming Flesh* by Horace Hummel (St. Louis: Concordia, 1979) also contains much that is of value for the proper interpretation of this biblical book.

Dating of Job

The Book of Job contains characteristics of literature from the second millennium B.C. However, the work itself does not specify the dates of Job's life or of the writing of his biography. Some literary features in Job, such as archaic Hebrew words and patriarchal characteristics (long life, wealth measured in cattle, sacrifices made for children), mark the person of Job as a contemporary of the patriarchs. Also, the prose-poetry-prose literary structure in which Job was written was not unknown in Egypt, Mesopotamia, and Akkadia during the second millennium B.C. However, YHWH (the LORD), the distinctively Israelite personal name for God, is mentioned frequently in the book, which suggests a later date for composition.

Some scholars conclude that use of the word *iron* in several passages of Job (see historical chart) indicates that Job lived in the twelfth century B.C. or later. This conclusion presumes that Job could not have been familiar with iron earlier because it was not in wide circulation in ancient Palestine until that time. However, archeological evidence suggests that refined, smelted iron was in use in Iraq (ancient Babylonia) and in Egypt early in the third millennium B.C. Man-made iron products dating to the early second millennium B.C. have also been discovered in Turkey (ancient Anatolia). Man's use of unrefined, meteoric iron may date even before 3000 B.C.

The scriptural record states that Job lived in Uz, which was east of the Jordan River and included Aram to the north and Edom to the south. Uz was bordered on the west by the King's Highway (see Numbers 21:22), the second-most important trade route of the ancient world, leading from Noph (Memphis), Egypt, to the Fertile Crescent, making its way to Babylonia. Thus, it seems entirely plausible that Job, having access to this highway and being wealthy, indeed the "greatest of all the people of the east" (Job 1:3), could have had familiarity with the metal.

For that reason, this study places the historical person Job at about 2000 B.C. or thereafter. Strong similarities in themes and in verse between the book and Proverbs suggest Solomon was the author, although the Book of Job has levels of correspondence also with some Psalms, Ecclesiastes, Lamentations, and Isaiah. Following Luther, this study assumes that Job's book may have been written during Solomon's reign, which began in 970 B.C. Regardless of the dates for the historical person or the writing about him, Job's book is God's divinely inspired Word.

Group Bible Study

Group Bible study means mutual learning from one another under the guidance of a leader. The Bible is an inexhaustible resource. No one person can discover all it has to offer. In any class many eyes see many things, things that can be applied to many life situations. The leader should resist the temptation to "give the answers" and so act as an "authority." This teaching approach stifles participation by individual members and can actually hamper learning. As a general rule don't "give interpretation," instead "develop interpreters." In other words, don't explain what the learners can discover by themselves. This is not to say that the leader shouldn't share insights and information gained by his or her class members during the lesson, or engage them in meaningful sharing and discussion or lead them to a summary of the lesson at the close.

Have a chalkboard and chalk or newsprint and marker available to emphasize significant points of the lesson. Rephrase your inquiries or the inquiries of participants as questions, problems, or issues. This provokes thought. Keep discussion to the point. List on the chalkboard or newsprint the answers given. Then determine the most vital points made in the discussion. Ask additional questions to fill gaps.

The aim of every Bible study is to help people grow spiritually, not merely in biblical and theological knowledge, but in Christian thinking and living. This means growth in Christian attitudes, insights, and skills for Christian living. The focus of this course must be the church and the world of our day. The guiding question will be this: What does the Lord teach us for life today through the Book of Job?

Teaching the Old Testament

Teaching the Old Testament can degenerate into mere moralizing in which "do-goodism" becomes a substitute for the Gospel and sanctification gets confused with justification. Actually the justified sinner is not moved by God's Law but by God's grace to a totally new life. His or her faith in Christ is always at work in every context of life. Meaningful personal Christianity consists of faith flowing from God's grace in Christ and is evidenced in love for other people. Having experienced God's free grace and forgiveness, the Christian daily works in his or her world to reflect the will of God for humanity in every area of human endeavor.

The Christian leader is Gospel oriented, not Law oriented. He or she distinguishes Law from Gospel. Both are needed. There is no clear Gospel unless we first have been crushed by the Law and see our sinfulness. There is no genuine Christianity where faith is not followed by a life pleasing to God. In fact, genuine faith is inseparable from life. The Gospel alone creates in us the new heart that causes us to love God and our neighbor.

When Christians teach the Old Testament, they do not teach it as a "law-book," but instead as books containing both Law and Gospel. They see the God of the Old Testament as a God of grace who out of love establishes a covenant of mercy with His people (Deuteronomy 7:6–9) and forgives their sins. Christians interpret the Old Testament using the New Testament message of fulfilled prophecy through Jesus Christ. They teach as leaders who personally know the Lord Jesus as Savior, the victorious Christ who gives all believers a new life (2 Corinthians 5:17) and a new mission (John 20:21).

Pace Your Teaching

The lessons in this course of study are designed for a study session of at least an hour in length. If it is the desire and intent of the class to complete an entire lesson each session, it will be necessary for you to summarize the content of certain answers or biblical references in order to preserve time. Asking various class members to look up different Bible passages and to read them aloud to the rest of the class will save time over having every class member look up each reference.

Also, you may not want to cover every question in each lesson. This may lead to undue haste and frustration. Be selective. Pace your teaching. Spend no more than 5–10 minutes opening the lesson. During the lesson, get the sweep of meaning. Occasionally stop to help the class gain understanding of a word or concept. Allow approximately 5 minutes for "Closing" and announcements.

Should your group have more than a one-hour class period, you can take it more leisurely. But do not allow any lesson to drag and become tiresome. Keep it moving. Keep it alive. Keep it meaningful. Eliminate some questions and restrict yourself to those questions most meaningful to the members of the class. If most members study the text at home, they can report their findings, and the time gained can be applied to relating the lesson to life.

Good Preparation

Good preparation by the leader usually affects the pleasure and satisfaction the class will experience.

Suggestions to the Leader for Using the Study Guide

The Lesson Pattern

This set of lessons is designed to aid *Bible study*, that is, to aid a consideration of the written Word of God, with discussion and personal application growing out of the text at hand.

The typical lesson is divided into these sections:

1. Theme Verse
2. Objectives
3. Questions and Answers
4. Closing

The theme verse and objectives give you, the leader, assistance in arousing the interest of the group in the concepts of the lesson. Focus on stimulating minds. Do not linger too long over the introductory remarks.

The questions and answers provide the real spadework necessary for Bible study. Here the class digs, uncovers, and discovers; it gets the facts and observes them. Comments from the leader are needed only to the extent that they help the group understand the text. The questions in this guide, corresponding to sections within the text, are intended to help the participants discover the meaning of the text.

Having determined what the text says, the class is ready to apply the message. Having heard, read, marked, and learned the Word of God, they can proceed to digest it inwardly through discussion, evaluation, and application. This is done, as this guide suggests, by taking the truths found in Scripture and applying them to the world, and Christianity in general, and then to one's personal Christian life. Class time may not permit discussion of all questions and topics. In preparation you may need to select one or two and focus on them. Close the session by reviewing one important truth from the lesson.

Remember, the Word of God is sacred, but this study guide is not. The notes in this section offer only guidelines and suggestions. Do not hesitate to alter the guidelines or substitute others to meet your needs and the needs of the participants. Adapt your teaching plan to your class and your class period.

Good teaching directs the learner to discover for himself or herself. For the teacher this means directing the learner, not giving the learner answers. Directing understanding takes preparation. Choose the verses that should be looked up in Scripture ahead of time. What discussion questions will you ask? At what points? Write them in the margin of your study guide. Involve class members, but give them clear directions. What practical actions might you propose for the week following the lesson? Which of the items do you consider most important for your class?

Consider how you can best use your teaching period. Do you have 45 minutes? An hour? Or an hour and a half? If time is short, what should you cut? Learn to become a wise steward of class time.

Plan a brief opening devotion, using members of the class. And be sure to take time to summarize the lesson, or have a class member do it.

Remember to pray frequently for yourself and your class. May God the Holy Spirit bless your study and your leading of others into the comforting truths of God's Christ-centered Word.

Lesson 1

The Pain and the Puzzle

Theme verse: *And the LORD said to Satan, "Have you considered My servant Job, that there is none like him on the earth, a blameless and upright man, who fears God and turns away from evil?"*

Job 1:8

Objectives

By the power of the Holy Spirit working through God's Word, we will

- delve into the puzzle of suffering: Why does a good God allow suffering?
- search out whether or not suffering can be good;
- grow in assurance that God rescues us from all suffering.

Before your session begins, you should read Job 1–2. Be sure to read through all the material in the Study Guide for Lesson 1, as well as the material in this Leader Guide.

Pray that the Holy Spirit may guide you as you lead this session. God enjoys working through His Word. Count on His blessings.

Ask a volunteer to read the introductory material in the Study Guide. Since many of the participants may not have read the first chapters of the Book of Job before your session opened, this would be the ideal time. Ask volunteers (only volunteers!) to read Job 1–2. As the Study Guide suggests, you may wish to divide up the reading between several volunteers.

1. Give a few minutes for members of your group to share their first reactions to Job's story. Ask whether his sudden and terrible losses remind them of anybody they know personally. Allow a few moments for sharing.

2. Ask one or more volunteers to read this section of the Study Guide. It lists several explanations about God and suffering—all from the world's point of view. Allow group members time to react and share their comments.

Then proceed to take a closer look at the text by asking volunteers to read Job 1:8–12 and 2:3–6.

3. Allow participants time to see that in both texts God limits Satan's power to hurt or harm Job (1:12, 2:6).

4. The texts show that God refuses Satan's request that He, God, strike Job. Evil and suffering are Satan's work, not God's.

5. The point here is to show that the evil against Job was limited; Satan could not use his full powers against Job. God set the limits and kept Satan within them.

6. Allow participants to share freely with each other.

Again, ask volunteers to read this section in the Study Guide. It is a summary of the world's ideas of why God, if He exists, allows suffering. Allow participants to share other ideas from the world that they have heard from friends, co-workers, or relatives.

Proceed to the reading of Job 9:1–14.

7. The group is asked to list some of God's mighty works that Job recites in this text. Job sees God as all-powerful over His creation. Keep the listing short, such as: "removes mountains," "shakes the earth," "commands the sun," Creator of the constellations. Obviously, Satan cannot perform these feats, so dualism is out. Deism teaches that God is unconcerned with His creation—a teaching denied by Job in this section.

8. Allow participants to share their views. Job is bitter, and although later he wishes God would leave him alone, here he wants answers.

9. Job is confused because God, who cares greatly for His creation, doesn't seem to care at all for that particular creation named Job! Expressions such as "curdle me like cheese" picture God as a craftsman who carefully and patiently constructed His creation.

10. a. This question may stir debate from those who think it is a sin to doubt. As leader, you will have to determine whether the debate is healthy or detrimental. If needed, you may point out that, unlike disbelief, doubting is not a sin that cuts us off from God, provided we take these doubts to God as Job did. It is all right to ask honest

questions if we seek our answers from God. (For an example of this, have participants read Mark 9:14–32, especially v. 24.)

b. Allow participants to share.

Request a volunteer to read this section of the Study Guide, and ask others to read Job 1:1, 8; and 2:3.

11. The texts show that God disagrees with the three friends of Job. Job was "blameless," "upright," and "feared God and turned away from evil." No one else on earth was like him. God does not say Job was sinless—but blameless, that is, forgiven through faith in God's grace, and leading a sanctified life of faith.

This is a vitally important point! Unless we understand that Job was blameless, and that innocent people like him can suffer, we will never understand the Book of Job.

12. a. Allow participants to share. Some of the viewpoints listed in the Study Guide are widespread. But on the basis of the texts listed, there is no support for the view that Job was self-centered or self-righteous.

b. Allow participants to share.

13. Allow participants to share. This question will be addressed in a later session. Don't spend too much time with it here. But you may point out that during his suffering Job seemed to move farther away from God, but at the end he is closer than ever to God.

14. God does not punish believers for not being sinless! Although we deserve both temporal and eternal punishment (and Job would agree), God's punishment for our sin took place on Calvary. God's hammer of justice against sin fell on His own Son. Jesus suffered and died as payment. When it comes to paying for our sin and sinfulness, Jesus said it best: "It is finished" (John 19:30). "There is therefore now no condemnation for those who are in Christ Jesus" (Romans 8:1).

Ask a volunteer to read this section. Jesus states emphatically that He must suffer and rise from the dead victoriously in order to accomplish our salvation. The attempt to prevent Him from suffering was the work of the devil.

Christians must deny themselves and bear their crosses before sharing in His glorious resurrection. Those who so lose their lives for Christ will find eternal life in His kingdom. "Through many tribulations we must enter the kingdom of God" (Acts 14:22). Note that Christians do not suffer as punishment for sin or to pay for our sins—Christ has already done that—but God permits us to suffer as He graciously leads us to glory.

15. Allow participants time to share their reactions to the discussion prompts at the end of this section.

Encourage participants to read Job 3–9 this week.

Lesson 2

Looking into Secret Sins
Part 1

Theme verse: *Then Eliphaz the Temanite answered and said: "Remember: who that was innocent ever perished? Or where were the upright cut off? As I have seen, those who plow iniquity and sow trouble reap the same. By the breath of God they perish, and by the blast of His anger they are consumed.*

Job 4:1, 7–9

Objectives

By the power of the Holy Spirit working through God's Word, we will

- examine the claim that suffering is a sign of God's punishment for secret or unconfessed sins;
- discover why it is vitally important to examine all advice we get in light of Scripture, especially if we are suffering;
- reaffirm that God shows us Himself, what He is really like, and what His will for us actually is, only through His Word.

Before your session begins, read Job 3–9. Underline those portions that might help as you lead your group during this session.

Read the materials for this session in both the Study Guide and the Leader Guide, looking up the texts as you read.

Throughout this week, pray for the members of your group, as well as for yourself, that your study of this Old Testament book will help your faith in Christ Jesus grow.

In this session, there is an opportunity to divide into small groups. If you choose this option, select small-group leaders ahead of time.

Share the material in this Leader Guide to prepare them—and to give them confidence as they lead others.

Ask a volunteer to read this section of the Study Guide. It brings in the widely held idea that God somehow speaks to us through the conditions we live in. In simple form: prosperity and good health mean God loves you; poverty and ill health mean God is angry with you.

Divide into small groups of three or four people each. In the small groups, allow participants time to react to the quoted statements at the end of this section.

Reassemble the groups into one. Ask for comments from each small group.

16. Guide the participants to see that God does not expect us to catch signals from Him through our conditions in life. God speaks to us clearly—not obscurely—in His Word. As Scripture shows us God's Law, we learn quickly that God is not vague about sin. Nor is He vague in the Gospel about the forgiveness offered in Jesus Christ.

Ask one volunteer to read the introductory paragraph in this section of the Study Guide and another to read Job 4:1–21. If your group is large, you may wish to divide into small groups of four or five people each. If so, share the following material with the small-group leaders.

17. Job apparently helped other suffering people before his own fall into tragedy. Eliphaz is criticizing Job for not practicing what he preaches. Ask: Is Eliphaz's point valid or not? Allow time for sharing.

18. a. Eliphaz believes in works righteousness—that our good works can make us right with God. If Job was indeed a good man, as Eliphaz still believes, and if Job repents, God will "owe it" to restore Job. Allow participants to discuss; then gently guide them to this understanding if they haven't found it on their own.

b. Eliphaz's view of Job does change! Later he considers Job to be a horrendous sinner, who deserves his suffering. How common is that attitude among us toward long-suffering people?

19. Allow participants to share freely.

20. If time does not permit, or if you do not believe your group is ready for a more challenging question, skip this question, possibly coming back to it when you do have time.

Ask a volunteer to read the question, and encourage participants to respond. Help them to see that the psalmist and the apostle Paul see things from the long-range view—in light of the end times (escha-

86

tologically—a term we will discuss in Lesson 8). Christians eventually do reap the benefit of their faith—a new heaven and earth—and unbelievers finally reap eternal destruction, but during this life unbelievers may prosper while Christians suffer. Job, a believer, had sowed in faith, but he was not yet reaping the benefits.

21. Ask a volunteer to read the paragraph introducing this question.

a. This part is frightening! In fact, it sounds spooky, because Eliphaz claims some special, direct insight into the mind of God. But it's not insight that comes from the Word of God. "Now a word was brought to me stealthily," he says. But God does not work in secret! "A spirit glided past my face," he claims. But this is not the Holy Spirit. This comes closer to the experience of the evil prophet Balaam (Numbers 24:15–16) than to any of the faithful prophets. The reason this is so dangerous is that claiming a direct message from God that contradicts Scripture is a sure sign of a false prophet, and whatever advice he gives to Job can never result in Job's salvation or good. The Gospel of salvation comes to us only through God's Word and Sacraments.

b. Allow participants time to share. You may want to point out Jesus' warning against false prophets in Matthew 7:15–23.

22. a. Bildad (knowingly or not) is playing on Job's fears. Allow participants to turn to Job 1:5 to see that Job sacrificed for his children in case they sinned. But there is no indication that their death was God's punishment for their sin.

b. Allow participants time to respond. For Bildad, nothing stands in the way of sin and its consequence—not even the forgiveness of God through Jesus Christ. To Bildad and those like him, the children's deaths prove their guilt. Bildad really has no hard evidence that Job's children sinned, nor that Job himself did. Remember, he only suspects they sinned. But even more important, Bildad knows nothing of God's grace and forgiveness—which lie at the very core of the Christian faith. The point is this: even if we have sinned, we can run to a gracious God for forgiveness.

23. a. Bildad believes that God takes us back under the condition that we are "pure and upright." He is in dangerous error because God does not accept us on the basis of our righteousness; God accepts and forgives us in Christ because He is merciful and gracious, and eager to forgive.

b. As participants can see, Jesus' words in Matthew 9 point out that Jesus came to call sinners to faith. He died to save all, but only those who repent of their sin and trust in His grace are saved, not the self-righteous. Let participants respond to how they would answer a modern-day Bildad.

24. Eliphaz's "revelation" is ridiculous. Of course, no one can be more righteous than God, and Job never said this, but Eliphaz implies he did. Eliphaz probably is asking the question to make himself appear astute and clever.

25. Point out that some angels fell and became evil, but unlike them, we fallen humans can be restored through God's grace. All humans are sinful by nature, of course. But originally, man and woman were created in the image of God. Granted, that image was lost due to sin, but in our Baptism, God re-creates us. We are new creations in Christ right now, holy and righteous in God's sight. Eliphaz cannot believe that God likes physical things, calls them good, and Himself would take on a physical body to become a man. Eliphaz thinks the physical is evil.

26. Allow participants to share freely. The irony that Eliphaz just cannot see is that God would become a man—in Jesus Christ! Because of the incarnation (God-becoming-flesh), God can restore fallen humanity back to Himself. We are told in Scripture that God sends angels to serve us (Hebrews 1:14), and we will reign with Christ forever in the new heaven and earth (Revelation 3:21).

Lesson 3

Looking into Secret Sins
Part 2

Theme verse: *Teach me, and I will be silent; make me understand how I have gone astray. How forceful are upright words! But what does reproof from you reprove?*

Job 6:24–25

Objectives

By the power of the Holy Spirit working through God's Word, we will

- examine the claim that suffering is a sign that God is punishing us for secret or unconfessed sins;
- discover why it is vitally important to examine all advice we get in light of Scripture, especially if we are suffering;
- reaffirm that God shows us Himself, what He is really like, and what His will for us actually is only through His Word.

Before your session begins, be sure to read Job 10–15. Also read the material in the Study Guide and this Leader Guide.

Should you wish to divide up a large group into smaller groups, select small-group leaders in advance. Share the material of this Leader Guide with them.

Mention the members of your study in your prayers. Some may be participating because they themselves are suffering. Your Bible study group can be God's instrument of strength, peace, and healing for them.

Ask a volunteer to read this section of the Study Guide. It is an introduction to an activity that might be better conducted in small groups. If you have prepared the small-group leaders in advance, divide into small groups at this time.

By giving participants an opportunity to cross-examine Eliphaz's arguments, they might be better equipped when they run into his arguments in today's world. While this might be quite easy for mature Christians, be sure to encourage anyone new to Christianity or to Bible study.

Go through the five steps of Eliphaz's argument. You may even wish to list them on a chalkboard or newsprint flip chart in this way:

Step 1: God is overwhelmingly powerful.

Step 2: God is even higher than the angels.

Step 3: God's justice is beyond our understanding.

Step 4: We cannot be certain God loves us.

Step 5: So, don't complain—repent!

Invite participants to examine these claims in light of Scripture.

27. Allow participants to share freely. Some pointers:

Step 1: Certainly, God is all-powerful and almighty. He can crush us easily if He so chooses (v. 19). However, God has revealed Himself to us in words and ways that we can understand. All of Scripture stands in testimony that God has told us about Himself and His will for us, and that will is good and gracious.

Step 2: God is higher than the angels, true, but God has come down to earth in His Son, Jesus Christ. God became man and lived among us to demonstrate His love. God used angels to announce His Son's birth (Luke 1–2).

Steps 3 and 4: We can know what justice is because God teaches us in His Word. God's wonderful justice is that He punished His Son instead of us. We know we are forgiven because Christ died and rose for us. God's love for us in Christ does not depend on our circumstances.

Step 5: In Psalm 50:15 God invites us to call upon Him! He promises to save and deliver us, to the glory of His holy name.

28. Allow participants to share freely.

Ask one volunteer to read the opening paragraph in this section and another to read Job 6:24–25, 28–30.

29. Some claim that these words of Job are spoken defiantly and that he didn't mean them. Job is certainly asking for straightforward proof, but there is no evidence he didn't mean what he said.

30. If Job was in error, he certainly would want to know about it. He would want to repent and return to the fellowship with God that he mistakenly thought he had lost.

31. Help participants to see that when our friends point out our sins and shortcomings to us, it is an act of love. Sin gets in between God and us. However, Christ bridged the gap for us through His death and resurrection. We are restored to God and His grace.

32. Ask a volunteer to read Job 11:1–6. Allow participants to share the views about Zophar. Zophar's religious fervor led him to fanaticism; hatred, not love, was the fruit. Zophar may be afraid of Job's probing questions about God; Zophar's version of God is smaller than Job's and is a graceless view. Zophar's views are not uncommon today.

33. Ask a volunteer to read the additional verses (11:7–12) and another to read the introductory paragraph in this section of the Study Guide.

34. a. Allow participants to share how Zophar misrepresents God. Zophar said, "God exacts of you less than your guilt deserves." Zophar meant it as "You, Job, aren't even getting all the suffering you deserve!" The irony is that, in Christ, God chooses to forget our sin, Christ having suffered God's wrath in our place. See Jeremiah 31:34.

b. Let participants share how they might react to Zophar.

35. Ask one volunteer to read the paragraphs, and others to read the biblical texts listed in the Study Guide. You may not have time in your session to cover all four texts, so select one of them to share with your group. (Direct your small-group leaders to do the same.) Ask participants how God confronts sin. God is open, not secretive. He pronounced judgment against it. He doesn't play guessing games with us over sin.

36. Refer back to the Jeremiah 31:34 text. God forgives; He will not keep our sin in mind when it comes to judgment, thanks to Jesus Christ.

37. Hebrews 8:1–13 clearly describes how Christ Jesus shed His lifeblood to redeem us from sin. On the basis of His sacrifice, God chooses to "remember [our] sins no more."

38. Allow participants to share.

Lesson 4

Suffering and Prayer

Theme verse: *There is no arbiter between us, who might lay his hand on us both. Let Him take His rod away from me, and let not dread of Him terrify me.*

Job 9:33–34

Objectives

By the power of the Holy Spirit working through God's Word, we will

- discover that a time of suffering is not a time when God closes communication with us, but rather a time when God urgently invites us to pray to Him;
- examine Job's style of prayer to see that our prayers can be bold and forthright, honestly talking to God even if we are angry or despairing;
- apply to our own lives the strength Job found when he discovered that God was for him even when he felt that God was against him.

Before your session begins, be sure to read Job 16–21, as well as the material in Lesson 4 of the Study Guide.

If you wish to divide into small groups during this session, select ahead of time some small-group leaders. This will give you time to share the material in the Leader Guide with them.

The suggested closing prayer involves petitions for specific people who are suffering. Ask participants at the beginning of the session to think of people they would like to pray for, and pray for the members of your study group.

You may wish to divide into small groups of three or four so that participants can better discuss how they pray during times of suffering. Discussion prompts are listed in the Study Guide.

39. Allow participants to share whether or not they think complaint is a proper form of prayer. Many of the psalms are laments or complaints spoken in faith.

40. Again, allow participants to share freely.

There is a good reason why Job talks more and more to God and less and less to his friends as time goes on. The friends were of no comfort—they did not speak the Gospel of God's love, but only Law and works-righteousness. So Job turns to God. The purpose of this section is to explore the reasons why Job did not start by talking with God in prayer.

41. (A textual note on v. 3. Some versions read the opposite way, saying that if we would sue God, He would not answer one question in a thousand. If different readings appear in the Bibles your group uses, you might point out that, ultimately, it comes down to the same thing: We would be put on the spot, not God.)

Allow participants to respond freely. Job is feeling the weight of the Law. Any of us, if we are living under Law, would hate to be scrutinized by God. Here is one clue about Job's hesitancy to pray: he seems to have forgotten that he is living under grace.

42. Allow participants to share answers. The formula for prayer suggested by Job's friends sounds like a how-to course. It's based on two false notions: (1) works-righteousness and (2) that God must act in a prescribed way—that we can "get God to do something." But God is just too big! Job's God is far bigger than the friends' view. And Job's faith is much bigger too.

43. a. Allow participants to share their views. Job isn't discounting mercy—the God he knows is a merciful God. The trouble is that Job's experience isn't meshing with what he knows about God. That's why it's vindication he wants.

b. Allow your group to wrestle with this one, sharing freely. There will be practical application of this in the following discussion question.

44. This question is tied into the previous one. Allow participants to respond. If they are having difficulties, guide them to see that God doesn't want contrived confessions. A dishonest confession of sin is just that: dishonest. More than that, it cannot possibly honor God.

Rather, it would be making God into a bully who gloats that He's got us under His thumb. That isn't God! And Job knew it.

But there's even more to it than that. Even if we could be absolutely sinless and perfect, it still wouldn't give us any control over God. God loves us freely, not because He is obligated, but simply because He is a God of grace. Job knew that too. His faith in the true God was deeper than the friends' faith.

Ask one volunteer to read the opening paragraphs in this section and another to read Job 9:32–35. This is one of the most significant texts in the Book of Job.

45. Allow participants time to see that Job fears that God's power will be used to hurt him. Job wants reassurance of God's love, not God's power.

46. Ask someone to read this paragraph, and be sure that everybody comprehends just what it is Job is asking for: a referee between him and God.

a. Members of your group probably will see that a referee with no authority or power over the two sides (or players) is not going to be a very helpful referee. Ask: Do we see why Job's referee has to be as strong as God?

b. Allow participants to share as the Study Guide suggests.

47. Ask a volunteer to record the group's suggestions of qualifications a referee must have. Of course, we are leading up to Jesus Christ being our referee. Jesus is true God, so His death alone has the power to turn God's anger at our sin into love for us. Jesus is true man, so He can sympathize with us and represent us before God. He alone can reconcile us to God, bringing us together in peace.

Read the opening sentence in the Study Guide, and ask a volunteer to read Job 10.

48. Participants will see in verse 2 that Job says, "I will say to God." Then, immediately in verse 3, Job addresses God Himself. Notice the use of the second person—"You."

49. Allow participants to share. What changed was this: Job realized by faith that he had just what he asked for. Now he can talk to God without fear. Job reaffirms his faith in this referee later (16:19–21; 19:25).

50. Let participants check the Isaiah 52–53 and Galatians 3 texts. Both show that Christ Jesus, God's Son, removed the rod from us and

let it fall on Himself. We simply do not have to fear God's wrath any longer.

This section is not a "how-to" minicourse on prayer. But by looking into this part of the Book of Job, we can see how we are free to pray to our heavenly Father.

Ask a volunteer to read the opening paragraphs and ask for any comments. Point out that we do have an arbiter/referee, Jesus.

51. Allow participants to rate how open Job's prayer was.

52. Jesus is God's only-begotten Son, God Himself. He is equally God with the Father and the Spirit. But Jesus also became man, put on human flesh, and was/is fully a man. He is both God and man. There can't be any better go-between.

53. Allow participants to share responses with one another. *Sym* in Greek means "with." And the root *path* means "suffer." Therefore, *sympathy* means "to suffer with."

54. Allow participants as much time as possible to share how their prayers might become bolder. We can lament to God, sharing with God anything that is on our hearts; He hears it all with sympathy.

Lesson 5

Christ to the Rescue

Theme verse: *Even now, behold, my witness is in heaven, and He who testifies for me is on high. My friends scorn me; my eye pours out tears to God, that He would argue the case of a man with God, as a son of man does with his neighbor.*

Job 16:19–21

Objectives

By the power of the Holy Spirit working through God's Word, we will

- come to see the preeminent place that Christ Jesus plays in the Book of Job;
- grow, as Job did, to depend thoroughly on Christ as our mediator, especially at times when we may doubt the heavenly Father's love toward us;
- take comfort in the certainty that while our suffering is temporary, Christ's rescue brings us to eternal joy.

Be sure to read Job 22–25. Also read through the material in the Study Guide, Lesson 5, as well as the material in the Leader Guide.

If you divide a large group into small groups so that people will have better opportunity to participate, select small-group leaders in advance. Share any helpful material from this Leader Guide with them.

Be sensitive to the needs of those who participate. Christ's people carry each other's burdens. Tell your group members that they may feel free to share, since your group considers it a joy and honor to help each other. Mention these concerns in your prayers.

Ask a volunteer to read the scenario in this section of the Study Guide. It's not fiction. Cornelis, who endured suffering under Nazi occupation, is known by and related to the author. His views are merely representative of many who endured that bleak time in history. One of the two official state churches of the Netherlands subscribes to the teaching that everything that happens is due to the will of the sovereign God. The Lutheran church points out that although God foreknows all things, that doesn't mean He wills or causes all things.

Move immediately to the discussion prompts.

55. Allow participants to share how they might respond to Cornelis's view.

56. Job may not realize he is on a pilgrimage, but he is. And at this point in the text, Job is still under the impression that God willed him to suffer. The discussion question asks participants to give possible reasons why Job did not abandon his faith in God. One hint may be that Job firmly believed that God was also His Arbiter/Redeemer (Job 9:32–35 and 19:25–27).

Ask a volunteer to read this section in the Study Guide. It may help to underscore the fact that Job is very confused, but it's a confusion often found in those who suffer. The point is that Job clings to the belief that, in spite of the circumstances, somehow God is still for him.

57. Allow participants to share how having a mediator with God can help us. (One reason: A mediator can plead with God on our behalf—and can do so as God's equal—because the mediator is God, God's Son.)

58. Job recites a long list of charges against God. God tears him and "gnashed His teeth" at him; He is Job's opponent (v. 9). He turned Job over to evil men (Who: the thieves or the friends [v. 11]?). All was well, but now God dashes Job to pieces (v. 12). The list continues through verse 14.

59. a. Allow participants to share their views. Was Job sinning by charging God? The question is not academic. If we feel God has treated us without justice, how do we handle it? Help participants to see that God desires us to bring even our doubts and anger to Him. God changed Job's mind not by punishing him for his anger and doubt, but by showing him that He loves him and works all things for the good of those who believe in Him.

b. Again, allow participants to share. You may wish to point out that if we harbor ill feelings toward God, He invites us not to hide from Him, but to bring the whole matter to Him and ask Him to change our minds through His love in Jesus Christ.

60. Participants will see that after Cain murdered Abel, the younger man's blood cried out for justice. If God knows when even a sparrow falls, certainly He is vitally concerned about the lives of all His people. God's concern may be hidden in our circumstances, but His Word reveals it. Allow participants to share.

61. Some of the other actions Job mentions are "He . . . testifies for me" (v. 19) and "He would argue the case of a man with God" (v. 21).

62. Although the titles and the descriptions are not hard and fast, a suggested way of joining them might be: a. advocate, b. intercessor, c. intercessor or advocate, d. friend.

63. "As a son of man does with his neighbor" (v. 21) perfectly describes Jesus Christ, the Son of God who became man. The Hebrews verses below will illustrate this even further.

The Hebrews 2 text is one of the most comforting in Scripture when it describes why Jesus is the most effective witness we could pray for. Invite participants to work through the exercise.

a. Jesus destroyed Satan and death's power.

b. Abraham's offspring, which refers to Abraham's spiritual descendants: us.

c. The Father has a faithful High Priest, and we have propitiation—full forgiveness—for all sin. (We also have a Brother [v. 17].)

d. We have someone who went through suffering as we do and, therefore, understands and sympathizes.

64. Allow participants to share. If they need help lead them to see that the Father's love for the Son compels Him to respond to the Son's pleas on our behalf. God does respond! Ask how this might change the way they pray.

Ask a volunteer to read the opening paragraph in this section of the Study Guide.

65. God still dwells with us today. He comes to us through His Word, the Bible, and the Sacraments, Baptism and Communion. Christ's body and blood are even with us sacramentally in Holy Communion. Through these means of grace, God takes up residence in our hearts.

66. Certainly, God is sovereign and sits on the throne in heaven. But many who overemphasize God's sovereignty make an error. They believe that everything that happens is God's will; then they cannot understand why evil happens.

67. What God is really like cannot be seen by looking at what happens around us. What God is really like is seen only when we look at His Son's "throne," the one made of wood on Calvary. That is God suffering—with us, for us. And only love could move Him to do that. Allow participants to share their responses and views.

Lesson 6

With Friends like These

Theme verse: *With whose help have you uttered words,*
and whose breath has come out from you?

Job 26:4

Objectives

By the power of the Holy Spirit working through God's Word,
we will
- use Scripture in order to evaluate advice "friends" may give us
  in times of trouble, especially if they claim their advice is from
  God;
- learn from the negative example of Job's three friends how to
  minister to someone who is suffering;
- take comfort and strength from the fact that Christ Jesus is our
  true friend who remains with us when we suffer.

Be sure to have read Job 26–31 by this time. Read through the
material in the Study Guide, Lesson 6.

If you divide the large group into smaller ones, select small-group
leaders in advance and share material from this Leader Guide with
them.

Keep the members of your Bible study group in your daily
prayers.

Ask a volunteer to read the scenario. As the Study Guide
suggests, Karen's counsel is a combination of the worst of Eliphaz,
Bildad, and Zophar. After reading, divide the large group into smaller
groups of three or four people for discussion. Share the following
material with the small-group leaders.

68. Allow participants to share freely.

69. Karen's own insistence that she was listening to Charr shows her impatience. She might have heard Charr's words, but she didn't read Charr's meaning or feelings.

70. Participants will readily see that Karen was off base on a number of points. For example: "Suffering is good for us." Suffering is bad unless God can intervene and turn it into good. "Suffering can bring us closer to God." Suffering can drive people away from God too. God can certainly use it, but suffering is not a means of grace. God does not bestow grace and forgiveness on us just because we suffer. These and other points will be brought up later in the session, so there's no need to spend a great deal of time here.

71. Allow participants to share freely.

72. The episode was designed to show that Charr was talking about Karen's view of God, not God Himself.

This section is designed as a lead-in to the exercises that follow. Ask a volunteer to read it, and move on to the next section.

Ask a volunteer to read the opening paragraph in this section of the Study Guide.

73. Eliphaz is telling Job that God is giving him the silent treatment on account of his alleged unrepentant sins. See Job 4:17. Remember, this is spoken immediately after Eliphaz claims to have some secret, mystical insight into God's mind.

74. Allow participants a little time to share whether they have ever run into an "Eliphaz."

75. The Romans text tells us that it's God's kindness in Christ that moves us to repentance. Eliphaz and his modern cousins think it's God's threats or our efforts to get back into God's grace by our own good works that set us right with God.

76. The Psalm 50:15 text may be more familiar. It's a great promise that we may call upon God "in the day of trouble." Ask: What does God promise us here? He promises that He will deliver us. Point out that the promise in Jeremiah 33:3 came to Jeremiah when he was literally in the pits—in prison—not unlike Job, who was figuratively in the pits.

77. Allow participants to share freely.

Ask a volunteer to read the opening paragraph in the Study Guide.

78. Participants can see in the Job 6 text that Job admitted he was made of mere flesh, not steel. Suffering people might take a light-

hearted "Hang in there" to mean they should be able to endure by their own strength. It is much better to share your strength by helping them bear their burdens and, above all, to share with them God's strengthening Gospel.

79. Allow participants to share. If they need help, move them to see that when our suffering friends seem to be losing their faith in God's goodness, it's all the more reason to stay close to them. Even if they express anger at God, it doesn't necessarily mean they have abandoned faith in Him—as we certainly can see in Job's case.

80. Allow participants the opportunity to answer first, and then read Proverbs 17:17. The key to truly helping our friends is Christlike love.

81. Allow participants to read and share how these great promises from God in Romans 8 can help.

Ask one volunteer to read the opening paragraphs in the Study Guide and another to read Job 16:1–4.

82. Participants will easily see that Job's description of Eliphaz is apt.

83. The phrase "shooting me with Bible passages" is not meant to downplay the importance of Scripture as we help others! Suffering people need to hear the Word of God spoken by a caring Christian. Eliphaz was missing love.

84. Job would find it easy to speak the way Eliphaz did, if they could only switch places. Those who have it easy often think (incorrectly) that they know all the answers.

Ask a volunteer to read the opening paragraphs of this section of the Study Guide.

85. a. Unlike illegitimate children, the legitimate children of a king would one day rule. As God's children by our Baptism, we will actually rule with and under our Brother, King Jesus. His discipline now is training for future glory.

b. Eliphaz's words, as true as they seem, do not show the link we have with God as our heavenly Father! Eliphaz's approach is all Law; there's not a shred of Gospel in his words.

86. Allow participants to share their ideas freely. It is true that God "wounds" only to "bind." He accuses us of sin by His Law so that we will see our need for His forgiveness in the Gospel. Yet there is danger in using this to explain all suffering. How can we tell if this or that wound is from God, the devil, or the sin in people and the world?

Even if we knew it was from God, is the reason to give us patience, discipline or correct us, etc.? We cannot know for certain. The three friends of Job thought they were wise enough to tell, but God accused them of misrepresenting Him (Job 42:7–8).

87. The chain of events described in Romans 5:3–5 is this: suffering—endurance—character—hope.

But it is the Holy Spirit who plants and nurtures that Gospel hope. You may point out that without the Holy Spirit working in the heart, suffering can produce despair, anger, bitterness, and other evils. There is nothing sacred or holy about suffering itself. Only God can use suffering for His sacred and holy purposes.

Ask a volunteer to read the opening paragraphs of this section of the Study Guide. Point out that if Job was stubborn, it was because he was holding on to the true God, who is much bigger than the god presented by the three friends. In order to see this, we will take a peek at the end of the story. Ask another volunteer to read Job 42:7–9.

88. The text shows God is angry at the friends because they misrepresented God—they put words into God's mouth that He never uttered. This is a warning for all people who speak for and about God with no knowledge of His Word, the Scriptures. Most important, we cannot speak only Law; we must proclaim the Gospel of God's love and forgiveness.

89. Imagine that! Job's friends, who spouted works-righteousness through the whole affair, now must live under grace too. What they despised in Job (who lived under grace through it all), they now receive. Those who urged Job to repent must now repent themselves, and, doing so, they are forgiven. Interestingly enough, by God's command Job acts as their priest and makes the sacrifices for them! Job is acting toward the three friends as their arbiter, their mediator. He is acting in the place of his arbiter and mediator, Jesus Christ. There is something very beautiful here.

Ask a volunteer to read this section of the Study Guide and another to read what is probably the most familiar passage: Job 19:23–27, the text of the well-known Easter hymn.

90. Participants will see that Job, despairing of this life, expects full vindication in the next. He trusts he will see God with his own eyes; he believes in the resurrection of the body and the life everlasting. This is the best and only comfort for those grieving the death of a believer.

91. Allow participants to rejoice over this promise! Romans 8:1 shows that there is no condemnation for those who live and die with faith in Jesus Christ.

92. Even though the people had strayed from God, Jesus faithfully ministered to them. There are many cases of this, but only three are listed. Feel free to add your own. Matthew 9:35–36 powerfully shows Jesus' compassion on the crowds and His desire to be their Shepherd, to care for them. Romans 5:6–8 shows that God's love is not conditional, not based on our love for Him! Even when we were God's enemies, He demonstrated His love by dying for us. 2 Timothy 2:13 emphatically shows that even if we are faithless, Jesus remains faithful to us; that is His very nature.

93. Allow participants to share how these insights into what Christ Jesus is like can help them.

Lesson 7

Where Is God
When I Need Him?

Theme Verse: *Oh, that I knew where I might find Him,*
that I might come even to His seat!

Job 23:3

Objectives

By the power of the Holy Spirit working through God's Word, we will

- examine Job's complaint that God hides Himself from the suffering person;
- see from God's own speeches to Job that God will never abandon His people to the forces of evil, knowing better than we do that we could never survive on our own without Him;
- hear God's gracious invitation to be still and know that He is God our Father.

Before your session begins, be sure to read Job 32–37. Read through the material in the Study Guide, Lesson 7. If you find the material too lengthy, cross out those sections that you feel your group should skip.

If you are going to break the large group into smaller groups, assign small-group leaders beforehand. Share the material in this Leader Guide with them.

By now your large group and small groups probably have worked well together and share more freely than they did at the beginning. Be prepared to allow members to share their hurts with others. Keep them in your prayers.

Ask a volunteer to read the opening paragraphs of this section in the Study Guide. It introduces a new scene in the drama of the Book of Job: the entrance of a new friend, Elihu.

Although the Study Guide suggests that you ask a volunteer to read Job 32:1–22, this section could become lengthy. Feel free to skip this section if you are pressed for time. Otherwise, proceed with the following.

94. Allow participants freedom to describe Elihu as they see him. He is certainly a better friend to Job than the others, and his words ring truer. Yet, Elihu is indeed "full of words," as he says (Job 32:18); we'd say verbose. He feels he has all the answers, and he is self-confident. However, allow participants to call it as they see it. Ask whether or not they think Elihu will be a good comforter for Job.

95. Let participants share freely. It is true that Elihu exposed the blatantly wrong assumption of the other friends: As time went on, the more convinced they became that Job's suffering was due to sin. They didn't know of any sin, so they made up sins to charge against Job. Point out that Elihu exposes a tendency many people have today: Out of impatience we, too, might assume that a person brings suffering down on himself or herself.

96. Reread Job 33:8–12. We may debate about Elihu's style or approach, but on this point he is correct. In anger, Job had wrongly accused God of injustice. But God is not our enemy; Satan is. In his own hellish way, Satan tempts us to think that it is God who is against us. As Christians, we must expose Satan's tactic to our suffering friends. Otherwise, they might not go to the only Friend who can really save.

97. Ask a participant to read aloud Eliphaz's speech in Job 4:12–17 and another to compare it to Elihu's in 33:14–18.

Members of your group probably will see that Elihu doesn't get into the mystical nonsense of Eliphaz. As should we, Elihu points to what God has spoken (33:14), unlike Eliphaz, who relied on a secret word from a mysterious spirit. But we cannot determine how God feels toward us by dreams or by our suffering. Scripture is the only reliable Word from God to us, and it reveals Christ, our Savior.

98. Elihu makes one tremendously important point the three others missed: God, indeed, is out to save us from falling into the pit (condemnation and hell). God's purpose is to redeem us. If He uses

suffering, it is only to drive us back to His Word, where He has been speaking His saving Gospel to us all along.

Ask a volunteer to read this section in the Study Guide.

99. Allow participants to share. Remember that some people may never have realized that the common idea that suffering is God's way of speaking to us conflicts with the fact that God conveys His grace and love only through His Word and Sacraments. Also, since success and prosperity do not necessarily mean that God is happy with a person; they can give a false sense of security!

100. In Job 33:22–24 participants can see Jesus as our mediator who spares us from going down to the pit (hell). The ransom He pays is His own sinless life on the cross. The result is that we have favor with God, are righteous in His sight, and have the promise of bodily resurrection (vv. 25–26).

101. As the text points out, Christ restores us to God. While Elihu has a wonderful Gospel message, he still implies in Job 33:27–28 that Job's suffering is God's chastisement to turn him from sin. We know from Job 1–2 that was not the reason.

102. Allow participants to share freely.

Ask a volunteer to read the opening paragraphs of this section in the Study Guide.

103. Participants will see that Job's suffering began when, due to a great wind, his children were killed. That storm was brewed by Satan. That must have impressed Job, for in 9:17 he says that if he ever met God, God would crush him with a storm. God may very well have come to Job in a storm just to show him (and us) that God doesn't come to crush us, but to restore us. "For those who love God all things"—even life's storms—"work together for good" (Romans 8:28).

104. Help participants to see that even as God points out Job's sin of speaking without proper knowledge (he accused God of being unjust and angry), God is at the same time remedying the situation. He uses His Word to tell Job what He is like. God uses the Scriptures, including this same speech, to tell us what He is like today.

105. Allow participants to offer opinions on how Job must have felt about God's invitation. Yet God offers us the same invitation to converse with Him. Isaiah 1:18 is one such invitation. Certainly, God has used your Bible study group as a "Come now, let us reason together" opportunity.

Ask a volunteer to read the opening paragraph of this section of the Study Guide.

106. Allow participants time to discuss this question. Lead them to see that by not listing Job's sins (as the friends tried to do) God is not charging Job with any sin at all! He simply isn't going to talk about it, because it isn't the reason for his suffering! This is pure grace at its best! Of course, notice that God does this in the presence of Job's Pharisee-like friends. This must have been very painful to them.

107. a. Allow participants time to read the text. The text certainly applies when we question God's justice and when we're tempted to think we can run things better than He can. God hints that even if we had His almighty power, we would not always use it for good as He does. God's ultimate purpose always is to save (v. 14).

b. Some commentators point out that this is precisely what God is asking. God's implied answer is that we would become more like Satan than like God if we had His power to bring "justice" to earth (vv. 11–13). God uses His power graciously to draw people to Himself.

Ask a volunteer to read the opening paragraph.

108. (Text note: An explanation of Behemoth is offered here that may not be the same as in footnotes of your group's Bibles. It is in keeping, however, with the best principles of biblical interpretation. See "Job and the Theology of the Cross," by Dr. Christopher Mitchell, *Concordia Journal,* April, 1989, pp. 167–68.)

Let participants share how this text can help them.

109. (Text note: Leviathan is explained in the same article by Dr. Mitchell.)

Participants will probably see the similarity between this text and Luther's hymn "A Mighty Fortress Is Our God." Referring to Satan, Luther writes, "On earth is not his equal." Of course, Luther implies what God says in this text: Without God, we are helpless before Satan, but Satan is no match for God, and in Christ we overcome Satan.

110. Allow participants to share their insights. If needed, help them to see that God is not trying to frighten anyone by describing the hellish forces so vividly. He is, however, showing that He is in control of every force in the universe and that we can rely on Him to slay Satan for us and save us from all evil. God slew Satan through the death of His Son on the cross (1 John 3:8). Jesus has saved us from sin, death, and the devil.

111. Participants will easily see the similarity to Romans 8:28, a text referred to earlier.

112. See "Gathering the Pieces" at the end of Lesson One in this Leader Guide. This difficult concept must be explained cautiously and carefully.

Lesson 8

The Lord Is Coming!

Theme verse: *Behold, we consider those blessed who remained
steadfast. You have heard of the steadfastness of Job,
and you have seen the purpose of the Lord,
how the Lord is compassionate and merciful.*

James 5:11

Objectives

By the power of the Holy Spirit working through God's Word,
we will
- see Jesus Christ and His triumphant return to earth as our
  certain hope;
- hear His invitation to rely solely on Him and His gifts (Word
  and Sacrament), and not on our own strength, as we wait for
  Him to return;
- apply the same comfort and assurance to our lives as God gave
  others, such as Job;
- discover the joy of Christ found in the community of saints,
  our fellow believers.

If you have followed the suggested readings, you have now
finished the Book of Job. Congratulations!

Be sure to read the material in the Study Guide for this session.

If you plan to divide the large group into small groups for
discussion, share material from this Leader Guide with the small-group
leaders that you select ahead of time.

Continue to pray for the members of your Bible study group.

Ask one volunteer to read the opening paragraphs in this section
of the Study Guide. Have another volunteer read Job 1:8–12.

113. Participants will quickly see that Satan thinks that Job only serves God because it pays to do so. From his own twisted view, Satan can only comprehend a selfish relationship (i.e., Job has a good thing going physically, materially, and financially with God).

114. Allow participants to share. Satan thinks that the moment God withdraws His support of Job, Job will abandon Him. Obviously, Satan projects his own hatred of God upon Job.

115. Allow participants to share their views. Even if they do not now, they will later see that Job truly repented. He never asked to get things back; he only wanted God back. (Of course, he had God all along; he just didn't know it.) He longed to hear God tell him of His grace, and was satisfied when God did, even before he was blessed again.

116. a. There is no evidence that Job repented only to be restored to his wealth, and so forth. In fact, nothing was restored until Job prayed and sacrificed for his friends!

b. Allow participants to share their views. Lead your group to see (if they don't already) that Job didn't earn his restoration by repenting. God restored Job because God loves Job, as He also loves us. It's pure grace at work here. And God wanted to vindicate Job in front of everyone (including us, via His Word) to show that He is a loving Father.

117. Again, allow participants to share their biblical insights. Throughout the book, Job repeatedly said he wanted his relationship with God back, and the words of the confession confirm this: "I had heard of You by the hearing of the ear, but now my eye sees You" (42:5). He never did ask for his property to be returned; he just wanted to know God still loved him.

Ask a volunteer to read this section in the Study Guide.

118. Lead participants into a discussion of C. S. Lewis's quote.

Although it is easy to agree to it while surrounded by fellow Christians, it becomes a little tougher when we experience envy of fellow Christians. For some of us, it is difficult to hold to the belief that God loves everyone equally when others have good health, talents, wealth, and so on, while we do not. DO NOT force people to share their feelings if they do not indicate they want to do so! But DO allow them to see that this is a common struggle for Christians.

119. Lead into a discussion of this point. The cure for our envy is found in the Sacraments. For instance, in Holy Communion Jesus gives

us His body and blood. That is everything He had to give; there simply is nothing better! The beauty of this Sacrament is that with our mouths we receive the body and blood of our crucified and risen Lord whom the Word continually proclaims. Allow the participants to digest that Good News.

Ask a volunteer to read the opening paragraphs of this section in the Study Guide. As promised in a previous session, we will take another look at Job 19.

120. Participants will quickly see that Job will still have what he has been wanting all along: his Friend, his Redeemer, Jesus Christ. Job isn't merely wanting life to go on. He wants life with God. Eternal life comes along with Him.

121. You may need to point out that God is not a materialist, but He loves the creation He made, especially us. He doesn't despise things physical, or else He, Jesus, would never have become a real, physical man. We know our resurrection will be a physical one, like Jesus'. Job stated clearly: "And after my skin has been thus destroyed, yet in my flesh I shall see God" (v. 26).

122. Ask a volunteer to read Habakkuk 1:1–4, a text which echoes Job. It is common among Christ's people to long for His return to set things right in a broken, fallen world. Allow participants to share their longing.

123. Allow participants to share as they wish. It is a strong temptation to desire the gifts instead of the Giver. Once we realize that, we can take that problem to a gracious God with a prayer of helplessness. 1 John 4:10 is beautiful here.

First of all, more important than our wanting God or loving Him, is the fact that God loves and wants us! That's the starting point. Over and over, He can move us by His love, which we see, feel, taste, touch, and hear in the Sacraments and His Word. As we hear, see, feel, taste, and touch God through Word and Sacrament more and more, He moves us to love Him more too. But it starts with Him.

Second, throughout this study we have heard that suffering cannot do what God's Word and Sacrament do. Suffering is not a means of grace. But when we are suffering, Word and Sacrament might sound and taste sweeter. If so, that is the Holy Spirit at work in us. It is He who moves us to love God more than things.

Ask a volunteer to read this section in the Study Guide. Like Job, we, too, may have more than we realize right in front of us. God is sharing His victory over Satan, death, and suffering right now, even as we suffer! Be sympathetic with those who may never have heard the Gospel explained like this before.

Ask another volunteer to read 2 Corinthians 4.

124. 2 Corinthians 4:3 clearly shows that God is hidden in His Gospel. The unbelieving world cannot see Him, because the god of this age, Satan, has blinded them.

125. Despite what is going on around us, and even the suffering within, Christ Jesus is at work in us. He has already made us righteous before His Father (justification) and He is working by His Holy Spirit to make us more like Him (sanctification). It's happening, even if we don't see it.

126. Allow participants to share ways Christians can help one another during our wait for Christ's return. The text mentions keeping our eyes of faith on what is unseen. Ask: How can we help one another keep our eyes open to God's love for us in Jesus Christ, especially during the bad times?

127. Allow participants to share how God visits us in Word and Sacrament, and how being with Him this way strengthens us.

128. Allow participants to share their insights into 2 Corinthians 5. Many of Paul's feelings are probably shared by members of your group.

Ask a volunteer to read the opening paragraphs of this section of the Study Guide. *Eschaton* is a Greek term that means "the end." Ask another to read Revelation 21:1–5. This is a view of "the end" of our story, so to speak. Point out that we know for certain that this will happen.

129. Both the Old and New Testaments picture the church (us) as the bride of Christ Jesus, who is our Bridegroom. As the Groom, He anticipates His bride coming to live with Him in His Father's house. The picture-language describes realities that are even deeper and more real than the words can express.

130. We will get God, and God will get us. Our relationship to Him won't be hidden any longer. Ask how this can help us endure our present sufferings.

131. Participants will recognize this text. There will be no sorrow and no tears after Jesus comes for us on His Day. Allow participants to share the comfort and strength this gives.

132. There's excitement in the text when it tells that God doubled everything for Job. The number of his livestock doubled. But notice that Job did not father 20 more children, just 10 more!

God is telling Job that his first 10 children are still his! They live, but in heaven. And Job will certainly join them one day. In fact, Job knows he has twenty children right now. It's just that 10 are currently hidden. Ask, as the Study Guide suggests, what comfort this can bring when we lose loved ones in the Lord.

This section is important; it gives closure to your entire time together. Permit the saints of your group to share how they appreciated one another as they grew in God's Word. Also, as the Study Guide suggests, allow time for people to share the strength they received from this special book of the Old Testament.

Purposely, we have held back suggesting the hymn "I Know that My Redeemer Lives" until this session. "Lord Jesus, come quickly!" "Yes, I am coming soon!"

CPSIA information can be obtained
at www.ICGtesting.com
Printed in the USA
BVHW051620151222
654340BV00019B/183